D0094903

**If I
could
tell
you
just
one
thing...**

"If I could tell you just one thing...

ENCOUNTERS WITH REMARKABLE PEOPLE
AND THEIR MOST VALUABLE ADVICE"

By RICHARD REED
with portraits by SAMUEL KERR

CHRONICLE BOOKS
San Francisco

First published in the United States of America in 2018 by
Chronicle Books LLC.

Originally published in Great Britain in 2016 by
Canongate Books Ltd, 14 High Street, Edinburgh EH1 1TE.

Text copyright © 2016, 2018 by Richard Reed.
Illustrations copyright © 2016, 2018 by Samuel Kerr.
"Breakfast with Bill Gates" text copyright © 2018 by Edward Docx.

All rights reserved. No part of this book may be reproduced in any form
without written permission from the publisher.

Library of Congress Cataloging-in-Publication Data available.

ISBN 978-1-4521-6515-8

Manufactured in China

MIX
Paper from
responsible sources
FSC
www.fsc.org   FSC™ C008047

Cover design by Vanessa Dina
Additional typesetting by Frank Brayton

10 9 8 7 6 5 4 3 2 1

Chronicle Books LLC
680 Second Street
San Francisco, California 94107
www.chroniclebooks.com

To Chicken, Moo, and Chipolata

CONTENTS

INTRODUCTION

A SINGLE PIECE OF ADVICE CAN change a life. It has mine on several occasions. And over the years I've gained a deep appreciation of learning from people both wiser and more experienced than I am. So ten years ago I made a simple promise to myself: whenever I meet someone remarkable, I'll ask them for their best piece of advice. It always seemed more worthwhile than asking for a selfie.

If I Could Tell You Just One Thing . . . walks the full spectrum of human experiences and emotions, from those of Simon Cowell at one end to those of Lily Ebert, an Auschwitz survivor, at the other. In between, you'll find the considered wisdom of presidents and pop stars, entrepreneurs and artists, celebrities and survivors; from people who've made it and from others who have endured incredible hardships, from those who've climbed as high as you can go in life and from people who've witnessed the worst of what humans can do to one another.

Good advice is like a nutrient-rich broth, made from boiling down the bones of life. And being fed so much of it, sourced from such remarkable people, has enriched my life and understanding of my fellow *Homo sapiens* immeasurably. If chosen well, a few words can capture and disseminate the main insights gained from someone's hard years of experience, thereby allowing us all to benefit from them. That is certainly the aim of each of the encounters in this book.

Every person is someone I've encountered either through running my own business, or from my subsequent varied career working in government, charities, the arts, and the media. Some people featured are friends, some are people who generously agreed to be interviewed, and a few are unsuspecting folk I ambushed when fate put us in the same room at a party, a conference, or, in one case, at a urinal.

When I ask people for their best piece of advice, I urge them to really think about what they consider to be most important. I put the exact same question to everyone: *Given all that you have experienced, given all that you now know, and given all that you have learned, if you could pass on only one piece of advice, what would it be?* There is something about asking people to stand behind just one nugget of wisdom that gets them to reflect harder, dig deeper, and be more candid in their response. And it has led to some extraordinary answers. The material is diverse and wide-ranging, and covers everything from achieving success to dealing with failure, from finding love to having better sex, from getting the best out of people, to surviving abuse. There should be something in this collection that speaks to everyone.

Most people, when asked for advice, are happy to give it. This desire to help is a manifestation of the better part of human nature; it costs nothing, can be shared infinitely, and will last indefinitely. And I hope that this is the first of several books, for there are countless remarkable people on the planet, and this first collection only captures the insights of a fraction of them. There are endless stories to be told and wisdom to be captured.

Over time I hope to help create a global commons of advice, a shared pool of wisdom that everyone can both contribute to and gain from. After all, as a species we are much more alike than we are different. And while everyone's path through life is unique, we can all benefit from the knowledge of more experienced walkers ahead, who can tell us of the most beautiful things to see and guide us to the safer places to cross the river.

IN THE BUBBLE WITH PRESIDENT CLINTON

HIS STAFFERS CALL IT BEING in "The Bubble," the experience of traveling in President Clinton's entourage. You ride in the President's plane, drive in his armed convoy, sit at his table. You don't so much as move, you *glide*. There's no lining up for passport control, no checking in, no checking out—it all just happens behind the scenes. You go wherever and whenever Mr. President goes. I got to ride in The Bubble on a Clinton Foundation trip around Africa. It was a grueling schedule: eight African countries in eight days. Every day the same: wake up in a new country, get in the convoy, drive hours down dusty tracks and potholed paths into the middle of nowhere, visit a project—an HIV-testing clinic, a malaria-treatment facility, a women's-empowerment group—then back in the jeeps and on to the next project, at least four times a day.

At each visit, the President was an unstoppable force: straight out of the 4x4, hug the local community nurses, talk with the dignitaries, dance with the local tribal performers, pose for the photos, do the speech, present the gong, stop and chat with the locals, play with the kids, notice the quiet one at the back, make a point of talking to them, give them a hug, coax out that smile. At every event. In the searing heat and dust, all day, for eight days straight. I've not seen anything like it. I don't think anyone has.

He reflected for a while when I asked my question about advice for life in a rare moment between stops. But the President's answer made sense of what we were witnessing:

> *"I've come to believe that one of the most important things is to see people. The person who opens the door for you, the person who pours your coffee. Acknowledge them. Show them respect. The traditional greeting of the Zulu people of South Africa is* **'Sawubona.'** *It means 'I see you.' I try and do that."*

Never has a person practiced more what they preach.

The craziest bit, back at the hotel, after twelve hours in the field, tired, dusty, depleted, when we mere mortals would be up in our rooms ordering room service and hiding, President Clinton is down in the dining room talking to the waiters, joking with the other guests, making an American couple's honeymoon, accepting an invitation to join a family's table, sitting with Mom, Dad, and two saucer-eyed children. He doesn't stop. He knows what it means to people to meet a president, or more specifically to meet *him*. And *everyone* is made welcome. Everyone is made to feel important. Everyone is *seen*.

"One of the most important things is to see people. The person who opens the door for you, the person who pours your coffee. Acknowledge them. Show them respect."

—*Bill Clinton*

MARINA ABRAMOVIĆ
IS PRESENT

'M IN DOWNTOWN NEW YORK looking for soup. Specifically, chicken noodle soup *with* prawns, or, I am now wondering, did she say *without* prawns? I arranged this lunchtime meeting with Marina Abramović, the Serbian-born, internationally revered performance artist, a month ago, and we agreed I would bring her favorite soup. I just can't remember what it is.

To avoid a potential faux pas, I get both. So when I arrive in the Greenwich Village studio where Marina works, the first order of business is to decide who gets which soup. Personal preferences are to be discarded; she insists on tossing a coin. Fate shall decide.

The fact that I worried she may be upset about which soup she gets both shows my hopeless Britishness and ignores the fact that this is an artist who has flagellated, cut, and burned her naked body for her art in public on many occasions. She is probably not the type to get worried about soup.

In fact, she is a woman who fits no type at all. She is gloriously, gorgeously unique and manages simultaneously to be sincere, saucy (she likes telling dirty Serbian jokes*), free-living, disciplined, reckless, and loving, and is about the most interesting and alive human being I have ever met.

In her performance art over the years she has pushed herself to the point where she has lost consciousness, gained scars, spilled blood, and risked her life. One of her earlier works, *Rhythm 0*, involved her lying on a table while people were given access to seventy-two different objects—scissors, a feather, a scalpel, honey, a whip, etc.—and told to use them on her as they saw fit. By the end she'd been stripped naked, had her neck cut, had thorns pressed into her stomach, and had a gun put to her head.

She has recently hit seventy and is more in demand than ever before. MoMA's 2010 retrospective of her work, *The Artist Is Present*, supercharged her international profile. As part of this exhibition, she sat immobile and silent in a chair for over seven hundred hours while thousands of visitors lined up, some overnight, to sit opposite her. Marina would hold eye contact with each person, fully present in the moment, reacting to them only if they cried, by crying too.

She explains that being present, gaining consciousness, is a big theme in her work. She sees cultivating inner awareness as the best way to disentangle ourselves from the artificial structures of society, so we don't feel disempowered or helpless. *"With many people, there is a sense the world is falling apart and it creates a feeling of just giving up. And that inertia is the real danger to society. People*

---

*"How do Montenegro men masturbate? They put it in the earth and wait for an earthquake." (Apparently a favorite Serbian joke about how lazy Montenegrin men are. With apologies to all our male Montenegrin readers. Source: Abramović, M.).

have to realize we can create change by changing ourselves."

This heightened consciousness can only come if we stop thinking and achieve a state of mental emptiness; only then can we receive what Marina calls *"liquid knowledge—the knowledge that is universal and belongs to everyone."* The mission to help people attain it explains her more recent work, in which she invites her audience to count grains of rice or water droplets, to open the same door over and over again, to *"create distractions to stop distraction, and rediscover the present so they can then rediscover themselves."* Given the originality and uncompromising nature of her work, the risks she has taken and the sacrifices she has made, it is unsurprising that her main piece of advice is a rallying cry to commit deeply to whatever it is you feel that you must do.

> **"Today 100 percent is not enough. Give 100 percent, and then go over this border into what is more than you can do. You have to take the unknown journey to where nobody has ever been, because that is how civilization moves forward. 100 percent is not enough. 150 percent is just good enough."**

I hugely respect the advice, but I reply that most people may not be prepared to put themselves in harm's way and in real pain for their passions as she has done. But for this too she has advice. *"Yes, the pain can be terrible,"* she replies, *"but if you say to yourself, 'So what? So Pain, what can you do?' and if you accept pain and are no longer afraid of it, you will cross the gate into the non-pain state."*

Advice I choose to accept rather than put to the test.

"Today 100 percent is not enough. Give 100 percent, and then go over this border into what is more than you can do. You have to take the unknown journey to

where nobody has ever
been, because that is
how civilization moves
forward. 100 percent is
not enough. 150 percent
is just good enough."

—*Marina Abramović*

TERRY WAITE, A PATIENT MAN

'VE JUST HEARD WHAT MUST be one of the most understated sentences a human being could utter. I'm having lunch with Terry Waite in his local cathedral town of Bury St. Edmunds. He is telling me about his experience of being held hostage for five years in Lebanon in the late 1980s, after having gone there as the Church of England's envoy to negotiate the release of existing prisoners. He describes his four years of solitary confinement in a tiny, windowless cell, chained to a wall. He recounts the beatings and mock executions he suffered. He explains how he had to put on a blindfold if a guard came into the cell, so he didn't see a human face for four years, and how they refused him a pen, paper, and books and any communication with the outside world, including his family. He reflects back on it all and says, *"Yes, it was a bit isolating."*

Terry Waite is the human manifestation of what it means to be humble, to serve, and to sacrifice. He put himself in harm's way in the hope that he could help others. And twenty-five years later he is still working tirelessly to help people whose family members have been taken hostage, which says it all.

The craziest thing is that he claims he was mainly doing it for himself. I tell him I know the concept that no charitable gesture is selfless, but this is pushing it. He insists, saying his career has been about achieving reconciliations, and following that path has helped him reconcile the different sides of his own self. He is also quick to point out that many people have endured far more than he did. He talks of people held captive in their own bodies, when disease or accident has taken away their ability to move. And he knows only too well of the many hostages who don't get to come home at all.

Both Terry's words and actions advocate the profound importance of having empathy: it is a fundamental tenet of his approach to life. He recounts meeting with the British mother of a man who was beheaded by terrorists in Iraq, who even in her terrible grief said that she knew her suffering was no different to that of a mother in Iraq who has lost her son through warfare or insurgency. *"In that simple statement, she summed up with tremendous courage something we should never forget: we are all members of the same human family. We all have fears, and hopes and aspirations. We all have our vulnerabilities, so we should be very careful before we attribute negative stereotypes to other people."*

Terry's empathy helped him stick to the three rules he set for himself when he realized that he'd been taken hostage: no regrets, no self-pity, and no sentimentality. He also stuck to his principle of nonviolence, a philosophy tested to the extreme when one day he found a gun in the toilet left accidentally by his guard. (Terry said, *"I think you've forgotten something,"* and handed it back to him.) So how does one cope with four years of entirely unjust and unrelenting solitary confinement?

"I did my best to structure each day. I would allocate a period of time to doing my exercises, then I would write for an hour or two in my head, then do mental arithmetic. And I spent a lot of time dreaming up poetry too. And then it would be time for some more exercises. And so on."

I tell him it seems it would be impossibly hard to fill all those lonely hours. In another world-class example of being understated, Terry just nods and responds, *"You know, the whole experience wouldn't have been so bad if they'd just let me have some books."*

He claims there have been unintended benefits of the ordeal. It gave him the confidence to leave his salaried job afterward and live a freer life. So one related piece of wisdom he is keen to pass on is that every disaster, or seeming disaster, in life can usually be turned around and something creative can emerge from it. *"That is not to say such suffering is not difficult and damn hard, but it doesn't need be totally destructive. It's the way you approach it, and the way you approach life after."*

Given that, what is his best advice for how to approach life?

"It's the same lesson I learned in that cell. What you have to do is live for the day, you have to say, now is life, this very moment. It's not tomorrow, it's not yesterday, it's now, so you have to live it as fully as you can. Invest in every day."

After speaking to Terry, I will.

TERRY WAITE

THE ELOQUENT MR. FRY

THE PREVIOUS TIME I SPOKE with Stephen Fry he was a robot. The setting was a tech conference, and he attended via an iPad attached to a cyborg-on-wheels, controlled remotely from a joystick and camera in his bedroom. This time, we're chatting in person over afternoon tea, sipping from bone china cups in a cozy members' club in London. The different interactions capture two sides of a fascinating man: on the one hand, a self-confessed techno-geek with an interest in the latest gadgets, and on the other a graceful British gentleman with a love of classic traditions and culture.

As you would imagine, meeting his real, rather than virtual, self is the richer of the two encounters. In person you experience his warmth and thoughtfulness, and a wonderful sense of complicity from the stories and confessions he weaves into the conversation. He's an easy man to spend time with.

Modestly, he says advice is something he is wary of giving, but he does have a few thoughts he'd be happy to share. I am expecting something literary or spiritual, but surprisingly his first thought is a broadsiding of life-coaching. *"One piece of advice I want to give is avoid all life-coach lessons; they are snake oil, without exception, and the art of stating the so-fucking-obvious it makes your nose bleed."*

I was not, it has to be said, expecting *that*.

When I query why, he expands further. One reason is *"their obsession with goal-setting. Because if I meet my goals, what then? Is that it, is my life over? I met my goal, do I just set another one? What's the meaning of the first goal if the second one has to be set? Or if I don't meet it, am I a failure?"*

As he talks, I subtly turn over the page in the notebook that lists my goals for the day.

Unsurprisingly, Stephen does not have a life coach. But he does have Noël Coward. And a quotation from him, which Stephen has above his desk, guides his approach to life: work is more fun than fun.

"If you can make that true of your work, you will have a wonderful life. I know how lucky I am to have found that, and how unlucky so many are to have not found that. People talk about work-life balance. But the idea of balancing one against the other makes no sense. My work isn't against my life—work is my life."

Of course, just loving your work is not enough; if you want to get anywhere, you have to be prepared to work really hard at it too. *"Everyone I know who is successful works, and works hard. Really hard. Maybe that should be my advice: work your bloody bollocks off."*

But the strongest recommendation Stephen has is to avoid the trap of thinking it is somehow easier for other people.

"It is never right to look at someone successful and think 'That person's got money, that person's got looks, that

person's good at cricket . . . so it's easier for them.' Chances
are, 90 percent of the time you're wrong. But even if it is
somehow true, thinking that is a very self-destructive thing.
It leads only to resentment, which is corrosive and destroys
everything but itself."

Stephen believes it is better to try and put yourself in their shoes. Imagine what life is like for them.

"It is the secret of art, and it is the secret of life: the more
time you spend imagining what it's like to be someone
else, the more you develop empathy for others, the easier
it is to know yourself and to be yourself."

Which is the best thing for us all to be.

"Work your bloody

bollocks off."

—*Stephen Fry*

THE EROTIC INTELLIGENCE OF
ESTHER PEREL

THIS IS PERHAPS THE ULTIMATE sign of the times: I am at an international tech conference, featuring literally thousands of founders of cutting-edge internet companies, but the talk *everyone* wants to hear is Esther Perel's, the world's most renowned relationship therapist and advisor-in-chief on handling intimacy in the modern age.

Esther is ready to speak, but the organizers won't let her. We're in the main auditorium, and there are 500 more people than there are seats. Founders are sitting on the steps, standing at the back, crammed into the doorways. However, the fire regulations won't allow for such numbers, so an announcement is made: until the extra 500 people leave, Esther can't start. But no one is prepared to miss out, and a standoff ensues. It's resolved only by Esther promising to repeat the talk later for the people who can't stay. In fact, such is the demand that over the weekend she ends up giving four talks. In comparison, the founder of Uber gives just one.

I catch up with Esther later, in her current hometown of New York. I ask her why she thinks so many people were keen to get her advice on sex and relationships. She explains, *"We have gone, at this point, into a digitalized way of life, a generation that has been clicking away forever, in environments that are sensorially deprived. And it creates a corrective need for human contact, for face-to-face relationships, but after the digital world we can often struggle with the imperfect nature of real people."*

The fact that people immersed in the online world sometimes need help with handling real life is not something she judges or condemns, but it is something she occasionally worries about. *"There can be something beautiful about the immediacy of connection that the digital world allows, but on the other hand dating apps where we swipe left or right can leave people feeling disposable, commodified, even, and that commodification is hurtful and degrading."*

Esther first received international acclaim for her insights into relationships when she published her book *Mating in Captivity*, an exploration of "erotic intelligence" and how to keep sex alive in long-term relationships. Esther brought into the open the underlying contradictions in coupling-up: the fact that we crave both freedom and security, the predictability that love needs, yet the novelty that desire longs for. The book gives some straight-talking solutions and has been credited with saving countless relationships ever since. Beyond the actual content of her work, the most fascinating thing is why Esther was drawn to studying people and relationships in the first place. *"My interest in people, in humanity, in the way people live, whether they create a life of meaning or not, it goes back to my two parents, who are Holocaust survivors. They both spent four years plus in concentration camps and came out with nothing. All they had was themselves, their sense of decency, and their* relationship. *That is what endured. And my dad said that was all that mattered.*"

And her father's wisdom echoes in the advice Esther gives, which is among the best and most profound I've heard:

> *"The quality of your life ultimately depends on the quality of your relationships. Not on your achievements, not on how smart you are, not on how rich you are, but on the quality of your relationships, which are basically a reflection of your sense of decency, your ability to think of others, your generosity. Ultimately at the end of your life, if people commend you, they will say what a wonderful human being you were, and when they talk about the human being that you were, it won't be the fact that you had a big bank account, it really won't. It will be about how you treated the people around you and how you made them feel."*

"The quality of your life ultimately depends on the quality of your relationships. Not on your achievements, not on how smart you are, not on how rich you are, but on the quality of your relationships, which are basically a reflection of your sense of decency, your ability to think of others, your generosity."

—*Esther Perel*

PEACE TALKS WITH
PATRISSE KHAN-CULLORS

P ATRISSE KHAN-CULLORS IS MANY THINGS: artist, community organizer, mother, freedom fighter. But there is one thing she most definitely is not: a terrorist—despite what some in authority would want you to believe.

Patrisse is one of the cofounders of Black Lives Matter. BLM is a peace movement that advocates nonviolence and seeks to never cause harm. It is a movement born out of love—essentially from black women who had grown tired, but had also honed a steely resolve from seeing family members being treated unfairly, often violently so, by the police and the prison system. It is a movement run by some of the most marginalized people in society: blacks, women, queers, the poor. It is a movement that seeks simply for society to respect the truth within its name. To label Black Lives Matter a terrorist organization, as it has been often, is as incorrect and twisted as calling Patrisse herself a terrorist.

So what does it feel like to be called a terrorist? I ask Patrisse. She goes silent for a moment. *"Disorientating"* is her considered, moderate reply. *"And totally antithetical to whom I am."* Then with the confidence of a person who understands the bigger picture, she follows up with, *"Of course, it is part of a long legacy of black people being called terrorists, when they are just trying to achieve equality in society."* As she points out, Nelson Mandela was on the FBI's list of terrorists until 2008 (well after he'd won the Nobel Peace Prize).

As a small but telling indication of the unconditional commitment Patrisse and her colleagues have made to the now global movement they created, she's making time to call me not only at 7 A.M., but at 7 A.M. on the Sunday morning of Thanksgiving weekend.

As we talk, Patrisse briefly describes her childhood growing up in L.A. It is a recounting that provides both the personal context to her mission and an insight into a dystopian parallel world of growing up poor and black, especially in the environment of the government's War on Drugs—a world where victims are often cast as the perpetrators, and the people who are supposed to be doing the defending can turn out to be the attackers.

Her childhood included the trauma of being arrested by police at school and put into handcuffs at twelve years old in front of her classmates on suspicion of possessing marijuana. She wasn't carrying any, *"but all that little-girl fear and humiliation forever settled in me at the cellular level."* She also experienced her older brother, a gentle soul with mental illness, being jailed on several occasions for nonviolent crimes. Subjected to both mental and physical abuse in prison, he was denied access to medication for his schizophrenia, and instead received solitary confinement and beatings.

Those personal experiences were the groundwater for her activism. But ultimately, a single inciting incident gave rise to Black Lives Matter: the death of Trayvon Martin. Seventeen-year-old black teenager Trayvon Martin was walking home one night, carrying a can of Arizona watermelon fruit juice cocktail and a packet of Skittles and talking on his phone to a friend, when he was shot by a neighborhood-watch volunteer, who was later acquitted of the charges brought against him. That was when the dam broke. And that was when, after the tears and the anger at the situation, Patrisse Cullors began organizing.

Because in Patrisse's playbook it is getting organized that counts. *"If you want to see change, you have to get organized. Stand for election. Win seats. It can't be just about protesting and advocacy; it has to be about taking power."* It is a proud, pragmatic, and positive statement, and entirely typical of Patrisse's approach. *"My story is not just about black pain and struggle, but also finding hope and doing something about it."*

There is no question that Patrisse is doing something about it. Black Lives Matter, which she cofounded with Alicia Garza and Opal Tometi, has in its short life become an international phenomenon, with chapters across the U.S. and beyond. I ask whether her work has changed the situation for black people. Is the trend positive or negative? Her answer is typically clear-sighted. *"It's both. There is no binary here. Are we winning right now? No. It is a terrifying time. This last year has been the worst year on record for black deaths at the hands of officers. But what is motivating is people aren't standing idly by—people of all ages, races, genders, sexuality, ethnicity are putting themselves on the line to fight against it.*

There is hope."

Hope is the internal energy on which any positive movement runs, and unsurprisingly, retaining hope is exactly what Patrisse advocates. *"It is too easy to become demoralized, to say this is awful and terrible, we're not going to get out of this. But we will. This too shall pass. It will be a blip in history."*

To ensure that this blip is relegated to history, her strategy of using the system, rather than fighting it, is getting results. *"In recent local elections, we have seen many black women become elected, some of the most marginalized people in our society are now in office. So there is progress."*

We briefly discuss another social phenomenon that has been in the press recently: men getting called out for using positions of power in their workplace to indulge in inappropriate sexual behavior. Could this be the beginning of the crumbling of white patriarchy? *"It's true that we're having a moment of clarity on this issue—people are getting fired, TV shows are getting canceled. But if we just get rid of the individuals and don't change the institutions themselves, it will go back to being business as usual."*

Gently, firmly, patiently, her answers tend to come back to the main point. Which is that we need to fundamentally overhaul the system; and you do that by building a machine, campaigning, getting elected, taking office. That is how you fight the power: legally, peacefully, and with an undying purpose.

So what tips does she have for people wanting to start a movement of their own? *"Never go at it alone. It's too important. We don't win things alone—we win in teams. So find others to do it with. Understand your goals and be clear on what you are going to work on. Build people's leadership and support those standing for things. And once you win, ask what's next. It's a long fight, and it is never really over."*

And her best piece of advice for winning the fight?

> **"My single most important piece of advice is stay healthy. It's too easy to become consumed by the issues that plague this country. It can have an egregious effect on you. People engaged in the fight lose their health, their mind, their lives. So do whatever you need to do to stay healthy—get a therapist, eat well, exercise. You need to stay strong, to stay healthy, to be in the fight for longer."**

And that's what matters.

"Stay healthy. . .

to stay healthy, to be in

You need to stay strong,
the fight for longer."

—*Patrisse Khan-Cullors*

MARGARET ATWOOD, AGONY AUNT

L OOKING BACK, I HAD AN itch of apprehension before making the call. I was due to interview Margaret Atwood, the Canadian-born, internationally renowned Booker Prize–winning novelist; a soothsayer and chronicler with the wisdom that comes from being over forty books old. To bone up, I read a couple of interviews online, but they threw up two uncomfortably pertinent facts: first, she hates choosing favorites of any kind, and second, she doesn't believe in giving advice. The reason for my call? To ask for her favorite piece of advice.

The phone call starts well enough. We talk of Pelee Island, a tiny gathering of land in Lake Erie, southwest of Toronto. She's recently been hosting the annual Spring Song there, a bird race and book-reading event that raises money for the Pelee Island Heritage Centre while drawing attention to the migratory birds that use the island to rest their weary wings. Margaret empathizes with them: the island offers her respite too, and a place to write with few distractions. *"The locals point tourists looking for our house 10 kilometers in the wrong direction."*

But I know I can't hide behind this island talk for long, so I outline my plans for the book, explaining that I am looking for her best piece of advice. Like all her answers, it comes quick and complete. *"Oh, I never give advice unless I'm asked for it."* But it's a better response than I am expecting, so I point out that I *am* asking.

Unfortunately, it's not the key to the conversation I was hoping it might be. *"OK, but what are you asking advice about? Advice needs to be specific. For all I know, you could be looking for advice on how to open a jar."* I explain that I'm OK with overly protective lids (run under a hot tap or gently hit the side to loosen); I'm looking more for advice that she particularly holds to be true or useful in life generally. *"Yes, but for who? For what? Advice always relates to the person and the situation. For a start, what if you suffer from depression? That can make a massive difference to how you are in life and what you might need or find helpful."* Ah, I wasn't expecting *that*. I know 25 percent of people suffer from mental illness, and I don't want to imply a sentence or two of wisdom will somehow solve their issues. So I tell her I take her point, and say let's assume we're talking about the other 75 percent. *"OK. So are these people born to loving parents or not? That is another huge impact on our lives and I think my advice would differ depending on that factor."* Hmm, now where? On the one hand, I agree that a few words of advice are a poor substitute for not being loved as a child, but on the other hand, it's going to mess things up for me and my book if I can't get a piece of advice out of Margaret Atwood.

I take some solace from her tone. She is not coming across as someone whose aim is to undermine—she actually seems engaged and eager to help. In fact, it appears she'll happily do *anything* for me, with the exception of one thing. It's just unfortunate that it happens to be the only thing I want of her.

I decide to call on God for help. *"Look,"* I begin, *"if you take religion, you can essentially boil its better teachings down into some human behaviors that are universally beneficial to all."*

"Ah, yes, love thy neighbor, forgive one another, that kind of thing?"

"Yes, exactly," I reply enthusiastically, thinking now we're getting somewhere. My optimism proves to be shortlived.

"Trouble is, I'm more of a revenge kind of gal myself. But when someone smites me, I'm normally too lazy to do anything about it. I tend to let karma take care of things."

OK, so religion didn't work. I try psychology. I give a simplistic overview of studies into human happiness, which show that people who help others end up feeling happier about themselves. Isn't there something in that?

"Sure, unless you do it too much, and then you end up exhausting yourself, and that doesn't help anyone."

I'm now starting to confront the uncomfortable truth that I am dealing with someone on the other end of the phone who is just plain smarter and of quicker wit than me. I'm basically in a verbal fencing match with one of the greatest writers alive, and, as you would expect, I am losing.

Margaret senses I'm on the ropes and decides to give me a breather. *"Look,"* she explains, *"I'm a novelist. In my world, everything is about the character. Who are they, where are they? Are they old or young, rich or poor? What do they want? Until I know what they are wrestling with, how can I give advice?"*

"President Clinton managed to," I protest.

Margaret's interested. *"Oh, and what did he say?"* I recount his advice about the importance of seeing everyone: the person who pours your coffee, the person who opens the door for you. I say it's a piece of advice that strikes me as something that's relevant to all humans. *"Unless they're a writer trying to get a book finished,"* she says, *"then I'd tell them the last thing you need is to see people more, you need to stay home and work."*

The conversation has the feel of a cat playing with a mouse. And I'm not the one purring. I resort to pleading: given all that you've learned, there must be something you think is worth passing on.

"OK, I've got something for you. How about this: 'When it comes to cacti, it's the small spikes that get you, not the big ones.'"

"Is that a metaphor for life?" I ask hopefully.

"No, no, I mean it literally. I was just in the garden doing the weeding before you called, and those little devils are painful." I explain that it may be a little too specific for this book, but I'll bear it in mind for a future volume on gardening tips.

I'm conscious that I'm nearly out of time. I give it one last try. Still wanting to help, Margaret asks me once more to pare down the audience for this intended advice. I confess that I haven't narrowed my intended audience down any further than to my fellow *Homo sapiens*. Margaret lets out a short, sharp laugh. *"But aren't you then just talking about a book of trite sayings that you'd read in the toilet, full of things like 'Make a smiley face and you'll feel more smiley'?"*

"Of course not," I reply.

But secretly I think to myself, maybe I can just use that.

"I'm a novelist. In my world, everything is about the character. Who are they, where are they? Are they old or young, rich or poor? What do they want? Until I know what they are wrestling with, how can I give advice?"

—*Margaret Atwood*

ON VACATION
WITH SIMON COWELL

'M SITTING DEEP IN THE stalls of the London Palladium
theater, watching four glamorously dressed people onstage
argue with each other. Above them hangs a huge backlit
Union Jack resplendent with the words *Britain's Got Talent*. And
beneath it sits the man who has most definitively proved that
assertion to be true: Simon Cowell.

After the judges finish play-fighting and filming wraps for the
day, I'm brought backstage to meet the main man. He's sitting
in the center of the room, surrounded by a bustle of black-clad
assistants, cameramen, and producers. It's the calm eye in the
middle of his own media storm.

I know his reputation for cutting to the chase, to put it politely.
I also know from his media director that he's twelve hours into
a twenty-hour day, so I am a little apprehensive, expecting a
terse, short conversation. But the exact opposite ensues and,
embarrassingly, for a forty-three-year-old straight man such as
myself, over the hour we spend talking, I fall hopelessly and
completely in love with Simon Cowell.

It starts with Simon sitting me down and making sure I am comfortable. He then offers me a cup of his homemade fresh ginger tea, but it turns out to be so fiery I start to cough and my eyes water uncontrollably. Simon is concerned and makes sure I am OK. Then, once he is happy I've recovered, spends the next ten minutes inquiring about me, my business, my story. He speaks softly, probes gently, listens intently. He invests more time just asking about me than the time we've been allocated to talk.

Eventually he allows me to move the topic of the conversation from me to him. His manner is so warm and kind and charming, and his voice so soothing, I totally relax. A lovely feeling washes over me, like being on a sunny holiday. He uses my name a lot and drops in the odd compliment. I get the impression he really likes me. I start to think we might become good friends. Maybe we'll even go on vacation together.

I catch myself. This is ridiculous. I'm a grown man behaving like a teenager. I need to concentrate. I push my man crush and daydreams to one side and tune back in to what he's saying. He's certainly someone worth listening to: a rich and fertile source of practical wisdom and insight, anecdotes and stories. I say his team strike me as exceptional in their commitment and professionalism, and he explains how he learned to get the best from people. *"Well, Richard, my dad told me there's an invisible sign on everyone's head which says 'make me feel important.' Remember that and you'll be fine."*

He's charmingly, self-deprecatingly candid about where his ideas come from, which makes me like him even more. *"So, Richard, I'm in my kitchen one night, cooking dinner and watching some boring program, saying to myself, 'I'd rather watch a dancing dog than this,' and then a few seconds later I think, 'Actually, I really would rather be watching a dancing dog than this.' And that's where the idea for* BGT *came from."*

I can see his assistants hovering, but I don't want my time in the sun to end, so I play for time and keep on asking questions. Given his dominance in the music industry, what's his advice for aspiring artists trying to make it? *"More than anything else, you've got to have a great song. Do small gigs. Listen to the crowd's reaction, find out what works."* And how does one cope with all the inevitable rejections? *"Listen to the feedback—you may learn from it. But if the people saying no are more stupid than you, don't get discouraged."* What if someone finds themself auditioning or pitching to Simon Cowell? *"If you get a yes, then shut up. There are times I've said yes and the artist starts with 'I knew it, we're going to do amazing things together' and the more they talk, the more I'm thinking, 'I'm really going off you.' The better ones just say, 'Good, call my lawyer,' and leave. That confidence has me reaching for my lawyer within ten seconds."*

I would keep going all night if I could, but I know that sadly, all holidays come to an end. And with local versions of his shows running in more than 180 countries, Simon has a long night ahead of him, with many questions to be answered, many auditions to watch, many people to make feel important. So I finish by asking for his number-one piece of advice.

"My best advice is listen—listen rather than talk. I was never bright in school, but I was a very good listener, and I still am. I have a better life because of it. When I meet

forty-three people, I'm curious about their story, about how they did what they did. Along the way you meet people smarter than you and they teach you what you don't already know. So I listen to them, take away my little tidbits, and off I go. . . ."

And with that, a final wave, and a *"lots of love,"* he's whisked off by his ever-faithful team. Unfortunately my holiday romance with the talented Mr. Cowell is over. I wonder if he'll write.

"If you get a yes, then shut up. There are times I've said yes and the artist starts with 'I knew it, we're going to do amazing things together' and the more they talk, the more I'm thinking, 'I'm really going off you.'"

—*Simon Cowell*

MARTHA LANE FOX,
FAIRY GODMOTHER 2.0

'M IN THE OFFICES OF a hip London digital agency to meet Baroness Martha Lane Fox, the First Lady of the internet. The company is full of people with ironic T-shirts, directional haircuts, and piercings that allow you to see through their earlobes. Martha's sitting in the communal coffee bar, looking gloriously countercultural by being dressed in a smart, powder-blue trouser suit. As someone who knows more about digital than all the trendies in London put together, she doesn't need to wear the ripped T-shirt and body piercings to prove it.

As we chat generally, I discover my favorite remarkable fact about Martha. It is not that she was the cofounder of lastminute.com, the dot-com-era–defining start-up that sold for half a unicorn. Nor that she was the youngest female appointee to Britain's House of Lords, impressive though that is. And it is neither the car accident that nearly killed her and resulted in two years confined to a hospital bed as they rebuilt her shattered body, nor that she now runs Doteveryone, her charity focused on making the United Kingdom the most digitally advanced nation in the world. Remarkable though these things may be, the nugget that best gives you a sense of the woman is her number of godchildren: she has nineteen. That's two more than Princess Diana.

When you meet her, it's not difficult to see why. She is alive with a sense of possibility, potential, and optimism. *"I love building things, I love ideas, and I love that you can always empower people and improve systems and make things better."* And her guiding philosophy? *"Without sounding too kooky about it, you feel much better as a person if you default to generosity as opposed to being mean-spirited."* What lucky godchildren.

Ironically, she herself has not always been on the receiving end of people's better natures. When her friend and cofounder Brent Hoberman floated lastminute.com and the share price crashed, she received more than 2,000 pieces of hate mail, *"including death threats and people calling me every name from B to C,"* as well as business journalists writing in the press that they wished they could shoot her, or that she *"should be put in a burka and told to stay in my box."* Not much generosity of spirit there. And, tellingly, all that vitriol was focused on her, not her male cofounder.

The lastminute.com story is a time capsule that reflects the internet of the late 1990s. They were ahead of their time, launching in an era before Google even existed. Their original name was LastMinuteNetwork.com but they thought it would be cooler if they dropped that third word. They struggled to raise funds because venture capitalists said people wouldn't buy things over the internet as no one would put their credit card details into a website. It seems laughably naive now, but Martha says it was a different internet back then. *"It was so new and exciting, a real sense the whole world was going to change, we didn't foresee that these huge monopolies like Amazon, Google, and Facebook would just go boom and lock down the internet."*

Her belief in the fundamental power of the internet to help people change things is the driving force behind her organization Doteveryone, which has the mission to democratize access to and understanding of the internet for, literally, everyone. She is mobilizing the government, businesses, schools, and communities to ensure everyone has the skills to get online and in a non-curated way. *"No disrespect to Facebook, but the internet is not just Facebook; if you know how to really use the internet, you have access to every opinion, piece of information, and tool out there. It can help us all change things."*

It is this spirit of wanting to improve herself and others, and of seeing the endless possibilities in the world, both online and off, that drives her, and it is reflected in the advice she passes on:

> **"Be bold. If you're bold you might right royally screw up, but you can also achieve much more, so be bold. You've only got your own reputation to lose and that's not important. It's much better to strive for something that seems impossible, that's quite nuts on some level. So be bold, whatever it is. Even if you work on a customer help desk somewhere, ask yourself how can I be bold? Find those small moments of boldness because they are everywhere."**

"Be bold. If you're bold you might right royally screw up, but you can also achieve much more, so be bold. You've only got your own reputation to lose and that's not important. It's much better to strive for something that seems impossible, that's

quite nuts on some level.
So be bold, whatever it is.
Even if you work on a
customer help desk
somewhere, ask yourself how
can I be bold? Find those
small moments of boldness
because they are everywhere."

—*Martha Lane Fox*

HARRY BELAFONTE,
KINGSMAN

I'M TALKING U.S. POLITICS WITH Harry Belafonte, the Grammy Award–winning singer, titan of the American Civil Rights Movement, and confidant of Dr. Martin Luther King. It's a big conversation. He is a man of extraordinary eloquence, intellect, and life force, the last being fueled by the twin engines of his anger at social injustice and his enduring love of the better side of his country.

We talk about the Republican primaries, which are raging around us while we're in New York. Donald Trump is given short shrift—*"a character clearly smitten with ignorance and arrogance, one doesn't need to linger too long on him"*—but he says what is worth greater consideration is the amount of people responding positively to Trump's messages of hatred, which reveals to Harry the extent to which the American Dream has been corrupted.

Conversely, Harry sees Barack Obama as one of the most intellectually gifted people ever to occupy the office but believes he's endured eight years of the worst animosity of any president in history—a fact that Harry puts down to *"one thing and one thing only: because he's a man of color."*

These two phenomena—Trump's popularity and Obama's received animosity—support his assertion that racism and inequality are alive and rampant in modern-day America and the wider world. And Harry shows no sign of resting while that is still the case. His work extends from fighting AIDS in Africa and serving on the Nuclear Age Peace Foundation to educating American students on the importance of nonviolent protest.

Harry Belafonte wasn't born into social activism or stardom. Raised in Harlem to working-class parents, his path to a life in the spotlight was precipitated while working as a janitor's assistant in New York. A tenant in his building, short on cash, tipped him with two tickets to the American Negro Theater. Watching the play ignited within Harry a love of the art form, and he decided at that moment to become an actor. He signed up for acting lessons and, to pay for them, started singing at night in a New York jazz club. But unexpected success there gave him the opportunity to launch a pop career, popularizing Caribbean music through his "Day-O (The Banana Boat Song)," releasing many successful albums of different musical styles and then forging an equally successful film career. All in all, not a bad outcome from a couple of free tickets.

Like many remarkable people, he claims his life has been shaped by such moments of happenstance—those chance events none of us has control over. He advises making the most of them. *"The greatest force in my life has been coincidence, and having an openness to receiving whatever the people I met offered and wanted. Due to this, my life opened up into a whole set of challenges and joys that I would not have had otherwise."* He summarizes this into one of his main philosophies for living: *"It pays to always answer the knock at the door."*

With his subsequent fame came considerably more of those knocks, including one that turned out to be the most significant of all: from a young pastor by the name of Dr. Martin Luther King, asking for Harry's help at one of his events. And at that first meeting *"Dr. King called me to help him with his mission, and there I was caught up in a social movement that changed the American political landscape and the global family."* He became Dr. King's mentor and provider, supporting Dr. King's family, bailing him out when he got arrested, financing the Freedom Rides, and organizing the March on Washington, and he has been carrying the torch for the Civil Rights Movement and other social injustices ever since. *"Those guys left me with my hands full."*

So, given all that he has stood for, fought for, and seen his friends die for, it makes sense that his greatest piece of advice is this:

> **"Discover the joy of embracing diversity. When people become more open to the strange, to the unusual, to the radical, to the 'other,' we become more nourished as a species. Currently our ability to do that is being manipulated, diversity is being looked upon as a source of evil rather than as a source of joy and development. We must recapture the profound benefits of seeing the joy in our collective diversity, not the fear."**

The most important advice I ever heard.

"Discover the joy of embracing diversity. When people become more open to the strange, to the unusual, to the radical, to the 'other,' we become more nourished as a species. Currently our ability to do that is being manipulated,

diversity is being looked
upon as a source of evil
rather than as a source of joy
and development. We must
recapture the profound
benefits of seeing the joy in
our collective diversity,
not the fear."

—*Harry Belafonte*

THE LESSER SPOTTED
SIR DAVID ATTENBOROUGH

A LL I CAN HEAR ARE the sounds of nature. The air is filled with mysterious chirpings and squawks, exotic whistles, tocks, and clicks. In quick succession, a Ghanaian Giant Squeaker Frog, a Madagascan Side-Necked Turtle, and a Pakistani Snow Leopard dart past in front of me. Then a Papua New Guinea warrior in tribal headdress appears. Our eyes meet. He gives me a friendly smile and comes towards me, extending his hand in a traditional greeting. And I think, not bad for a Tuesday evening in West London.

Admittedly the sounds are recorded and the animals are on film, but the warrior is very much real and enjoying both his first trip to London and his first-ever gin and tonic. We're at the Whitley Awards for Nature, an Oscar-lite awards ceremony for rising stars in the world of conservation. The venue is the Royal Geographical Society, an appropriate choice given the far-flung origins of tonight's nominees, each of which has dedicated their life to defending their threatened native species. The Ghanaian chap protecting the Giant Squeaker Frogs has even learned to mimic their mating call and does so loudly when collecting his prize. It makes for a memorable acceptance speech.

While the evening is shaped around celebrating these conservationists and their projects, the biggest draw of the night is guest of honor and the world's most revered naturalist Sir David Attenborough. He's dressed on-brand in a crumpled cream linen suit, looking for all the world like someone who has just come back from exotic travels, which of course he has. He's at the event to support the conservationists and wants no limelight for himself. Like his documentary subjects, he seems more comfortable hiding in the long grass and remains in the audience, avoiding the stage.

To talk to him one on one, he is the charismatic yet humble man you would imagine him to be. He says he gives time to these awards every year, including narrating each of the conservation project's films, because "*local people with local knowledge and a vested interest*" do the best conservation work and "*it's more important than ever to support those who protect the planet.*" It's lost on no one that the room is full of people inspired to do just that because of the films Sir David has made. The effect is global: President Obama credits Sir David with awakening his fascination in the natural world as a boy and asked Sir David to the White House to pick his brains on conservation and fulfill a childhood ambition of getting to hang out with Nature's commander in chief.

According to Sir David, the growing encroachment by man on our natural habitat and the ever-increasing demands we place on the environment has got progressively worse over his sixty years of filmmaking. And he's clear-sighted about the fundamental driver of the issue: "*There's no major problem facing our planet that would not be easier to solve with fewer people.*"

He also underlines the importance of appreciating what is around us: not just our natural history, although that is of course of fundamental importance, but also our art, other people too. He recommends what he calls an *"explorer's mentality,"* delighting in and savoring all the riches of life as we journey through it. And while doing so heeds, *"it's a good idea to create more than you consume."*

There's also a boyish mischievousness about him. When I ask for his best piece of advice, he feigns ignorance and says he's never been able to think of anything clever to say his whole life, and then winks. When I push a second time for his most valuable advice, he continues in the vein of what he has been saying about appreciating the miracle of what life on earth has to offer, and it fits exactly with the endless fascination he exhibits in every second of his films:

> *"I have never met a child that is not fascinated by our natural world, the animal kingdom, and the wonders within it. It is only as we get older that we sometimes lose that sense of wonderment. But I think we would all be better off if we kept it. So my advice is to never lose that, do what you can to always keep that sense of magic with our natural world alive."*

And no one does that better than Sir David.

"I have never met a child that is not fascinated by our natural world, the animal kingdom, and the wonders within it. It is only as we get older that we sometimes lose that sense of wonderment. But I think we would all be better off if we kept it. So my advice is to never lose that, do what you can to always keep that sense of magic with our natural world alive."

—*Sir David Attenborough*

THE REAL ARI EMANUEL

I T'S OSCAR WEEK AND ARI Emanuel, Hollywood super agent and inspiration for *Entourage*'s Ari Gold, is a busy man. He's so busy, even his assistant has an assistant, and she's worked marvels, getting me time with the most powerful man in Hollywood at Hollywood's busiest time of year. But there isn't a second to lose.

I'm grabbed from reception and walked quickly, almost at a jogging pace, to his office. A meeting is just ending, and this is our shot. Two people are still being shown out as I am shown in—we briefly get stuck in the doorway. Inside, Ari is standing at his chest-high desk, one that has been placed over a treadmill so he can work out while he's working. He looks up and over at me, then to his assistant, and asks, quite reasonably, all things considered, *"So, who the hell is this guy?"* And so my conversation with Ari begins.

If that makes him sound rude, then it's misleading. Focused, for sure. Direct, definitely. But not rude. It's just that *"It's a shitty week for me, what with it being the Oscars, and EVERYONE is in town, there is a LOT going on."* He talks in lean, rapid-fire bursts, all protein, no sugar. A dark-matter magnetism radiates from him; he's unquestionably the center of gravity in the room. He had me at *"So."*

Ari wants to know why I want him in this book. I explain it's about people at the top of their game, and that he's the most powerful and successful agent in the world. He listens to my answer, reflects for a nanosecond, and says, *"That's true. I am."* And then, a beat later, follows up with *"Well, it doesn't pay for me to be humble, not in this industry."*

So what does pay in this industry? What is the secret for getting to the top?

"I've thought about this, and my advice for success comes down to three things: be curious, show up, stay in touch. You have to keep reading, listening, talking, thinking, finding out how people think, what they do. And chase down anything that seems interesting."

He recounts an article he read ten years ago about a new technology that to him sounded intriguing and to us is now known as virtual reality. So he got on the phone with the person in the piece, invited him for lunch, and asked him questions. Ari kept in touch with the guy, sent him the odd email, the occasional article. The same guy called him one Friday night saying that he was off to see some whiz kid he was excited about and asked whether Ari wanted to come along. *"It's ten P.M. on a Friday night. I'm in bed. It's been a shitty week, pounding away trying to make this place work. But I think, right, fuck it. I get out of bed, put my trousers back on and drive an hour to meet this kid. Best thing I ever did. I loved him, decided to back him, and his company has been a huge success."*

I say it's easier to be curious, to show up, to stay in touch when you are already successful, when your name opens doors, so I'm keen to understand how he first got going, before his name meant anything. *"Basically I started out by calling the big guys in the agency world back then. I was a nobody, a pimple on their ass, but I just kept calling them and doorstepping them until eventually they gave me an in."*

I say that it takes a thick skin to keep going in a situation like that. He concedes that's the case and, surprisingly, says that the extreme dyslexia he suffered from as a kid helped him.

"When you're dyslexic, you constantly fail, nothing comes easy, so you lose the fear of failing, you get used to being embarrassed. So with cold calling, who gives a shit? They say no, big deal, you just keep calling them till they say yes."

Furthermore, he says being dyslexic teaches you other things too. It gives you better emotional intelligence: *"You might not be able to read books but you get great at reading people."* And it teaches you how to put a team together, *"because you can't do everything when you're dyslexic; you need people to help."* And ironically, in an industry that's typically about "me," Ari's reputation is for being about "we." The loyalty of his staff seems absolute, as is his to them. To illustrate, one of his colleagues was telling me how, during the terrorist attacks in Paris earlier in the year, as soon as Ari heard the news, he got straight on a plane and was there within twenty-four hours, making sure his French team was OK.

Curiosity. Not giving in. Team. All things instrumental to his success.

And it is one of his loyal team members who now gives me the nod. My time is up. As I'm shown out, I take a look back. The last thing I see is Ari going back to his desk, getting on that treadmill. And thanks to the time he's given me, he's now busier than ever.

"I've thought about this, and my advice for success comes down to three things: be curious, show up, stay in touch. You have to keep reading, listening, talking, thinking, finding out how people think, what they do. And chase down anything that seems interesting."

—*Ari Emanuel*

SQUADDIE BANTER WITH
CORPORAL ANDY REID

"*ARE ME FAMILY JEWELS STILL intact?*" That was Corporal Andy Reid's first question when he regained consciousness after standing on a Taliban IED, which blew off both his legs and one arm, ten days before the end of his tour in Afghanistan as an army infantryman. Fortunately for Andy, his future wife, Claire, and now their son, William, the answer was a resounding yes.

He tells me this when I meet him in his hometown. He has kindly collected me from the station, rolling by in his pimped-out 4x4 Jeep, with tinted windows, spoilers, the works. This is no typical disability vehicle, and Andy's is no typical story.

Back in his kitchen, while he deftly, one-handedly makes tea for us both, Andy recounts the time his parents first came to see him in hospital after he was evacuated from Afghanistan. Finding their son in bed, missing both legs and an arm, and with the remaining one in plaster, his dad, not knowing what else to do, patted Andy on the head. *"I said, 'I'm not a fucking dog, Dad,' and as soon as I said that we all started laughing and we knew then, it is going to be OK."*

To Andy, the jokes are "squaddie banter," the humor that soldiers use to lighten the mood and bring a bit of normality to situations that are often anything but. *"Four weeks after the accident, I went on a Remembrance Parade, and it was really cold, so I said to the boys, 'It's bloody freezing, I can hardly feel my toes.' It made everyone crack up and removed any awkwardness."*

The last thing Andy wants is people stepping on eggshells around him or feeling sorry for him. *"I joined up and I accept responsibility for what's happened to me, I knew the risks. That's helped me move on a lot easier. You don't move on very far by blaming someone else every time, it's just going to make you depressed and angry and bitter."* It's a way of thinking that shows the resilience and determination that makes Andy such a role-model soldier.

Instead of being bitter, each year Andy celebrates the day of the explosion. He calls it Happy Being Alive Day. *"When I woke up in hospital I realized I wasn't a victim, I was a survivor. Six of the guys from my company all died from one IED. I got to leave hospital after two weeks and go home, they didn't."* He says he needs to honor those fellow soldiers who weren't lucky enough to come back by living his life to the fullest rather than sitting around feeling sorry for himself.

One piece of advice he passes on to other people dealing with such a life-changing challenge is to remember that "the body will achieve what the mind believes." On each Happy Being Alive Day he sets himself a goal to do something physically challenging to prove he can do it. With this attitude he has so far climbed Mount Snowdon in Wales, run a 10K race, cycled most of Britain, and skydived twice, all things people would assume were out of the picture but which Andy willed into reality.

This spirit to keep going is evident in the giant poster he has displayed high up on his kitchen wall. It features a photo of Winston Churchill and one of his famous quotes in large type: "If you're going through hell, then keep going." The poster also makes it clear that Andy's journey has been extremely tough. He says not being able to run around with his little boy can really get to him and the pain can be gruesome on occasion, but he is resolute in his attitude of just keeping going. *"My little boy isn't going to benefit from having some dad mope about the house, is he?"*

He talks about his new life after the army. He is a man with a lot going on. He's a successful writer, with one book telling his story already out and another in the works. He's opened a café and bar in his local town, he got married, he's in demand as a public speaker on coping with adversity, and, most importantly to Andy, he can be around more for his young son, something that being in the army would not have allowed.

It's this new life and these achievements that give the context to his most important piece of advice:

> *"At the end of the day I think the most important thing is don't look back on what has happened. Instead look forward to what you can do. Just crack on."*

He is a living, breathing, walking five star example of that philosophy.

And his final comment underlines the benefit of his approach in the most indelible way. "You know, if somebody said to me tomorrow, *'Andy, do you want your legs back and the life you were living before?'* I'd say, *'No, thanks. I'm happier as I am now.'"*

"The most important thing is don't look back on what has happened. Instead look forward to what you can do. Just crack on."

—*Corporal Andy Reid*

SIR RICHARD BRANSON,
ISLAND MAN

FIRST MET SIR RICHARD BRANSON at his old house in Oxfordshire, where he was hosting a party the size of a festival in the adjoining fields for his Virgin Atlantic staff. He was the inverse of the protagonist in *The Great Gatsby*: standing at the gate greeting every person who came in, all 15,000 of them. For over four hours he shook hands, kissed cheeks, welcoming all—the embodiment of one of his management principles: if you look after your people, they will look after you.

These days, the place where Virgin staff dreams of meeting the boss is at his official home on Necker, his family's private island, nestled among the baby-blue waters of the Caribbean Sea. Every year, a few lucky Virgin employees get invited. As perks go, it beats free tea and coffee.

I'm on the island for a week, not as staff, but as a (very grateful) friend of the family. I can attest that whoever coined the phrase *"It's better to travel than to arrive"* hasn't been to Necker. Even the journey to it is epic. You fly by propeller plane to a nearby landing strip and board one of several speedboats, full of friendly crew, loud sounds, and chilled drinks, skimming over azure seas and nipping between islands until you get to the very last one in the archipelago, Necker.

When you see it, you can see why God kept Necker till last. two perfect crescents of virgin white, palm-fringed beach, trailing off either side of a verdant headland, upon which the proud main house inevitably sits. And while photos online might prepare you for the beachside Jacuzzis hewn from natural rock and calming infinity pools staring out at untroubled seas, what you don't expect is the overwhelming beauty of the wildlife: skies chaotic with bright birds of paradise, the lemurs' screeching calls for a suitable mate, an inland lagoon that's 300 pink flamingoes deep. I say this as a fussy, hard-to-please person—the place is literally perfect. It is where God would take his vacations.

It also affords an opportunity to observe one of the world's most revered entrepreneurs up close in his natural habitat. And if there is one behavior of this rare breed of business titan that stands out, beyond the generosity and affability, it's the sheer dedication of a man who wants to get the most from life, treating every hour as precious, a one-off gift to savor.

And if you don't believe me, this is his typical day on Necker:

6 A.M. Tennis with coach from Miami

8 A.M. Yoga on the terrace with resident teacher

8:30 A.M. Breakfast with wife, children, grandchildren, and friends

9 A.M. Kitesurf with son and son-in-law around the other island he owns (he's now bought the one opposite Necker too, because one island is never enough)

10 A.M. Head to private office with resident personal assistant

and broadcast-quality media studio to support the countless Virgin business and charitable initiatives across the world

1 P.M. Zip-line down from main house to beach BBQ with family and friends

2 P.M. Poolside chess with whoever is feeling brave enough (winner: Branson, R.)

3 P.M. Golf buggy back to main house to work

4 P.M. Second tennis session with coach

5:30 P.M. Feed lemurs

6 P.M. Necker tennis tournament with other guests (winner: Branson, R.)

8 P.M. Dinner by the pool

9 P.M. Party in the main house

All this is done with a flip-flop-wearing infectious enthusiasm. It's like he woke up that morning and, to his great surprise and delight, found himself in this amazing paradise, forgetting the fact that he's the one who spent thirty years creating it.

Over those thirty years, he's also redefined the nature of business. Before Branson came along, the stereotype of an entrepreneur in the U.K. was a wheeling-dealing Del Boy type. Branson changed that. He made setting up a business seem sexy, cool, fun—and, most importantly, possible. His success, life, and approach to business underwrites the ambitions of other entrepreneurs, providing a license to dream, to think *"what if."*

I catch him at one of the beach bars, at his feet the kitesurfing board he'd used to get there. He's talking with the bar girl making the drinks. He finds out she's going back to the U.K. but is worried about her lack of work. So he starts making calls, offering to help get her a job. It reminds me of a time when I was one of the judges alongside him on a young entrepreneurs competition. As we debated who should win, he made sure extra money was found so everyone would get something. The man is relentlessly helpful. The answer is always positive. His informal title in his own organization is Head of Yes; his most famous words, *"Screw it, let's do it."*

But when I ask for his most valuable piece of advice, it is not specifically about work and business, but about life and how to live it. Maybe it's the Eden-like setting we're in, or, more likely, it's because he follows his own advice that we're in this island of earthly delights:

> *"People talk about work and play as if they are separate things, with one being there to compensate for the other, but all of it is life, all of it is precious. Don't waste any of it doing something you don't want to do. And do all of it with the people you love."*

As he says this, I can see in the distance, one by one, his family, friends, and PA zip-lining down from the headland to join him on his private beach for another lunch in the sun. And I think to myself for the hundredth time, this man knows how to live.

"...all of it is life, all of it is precious. Don't waste any of it doing something you don't want to do. And do all of it with the people you love."

—*Sir Richard Branson*

KATIE PIPER, SUPER ROLE MODEL

I T'S A SUNNY AFTERNOON AND I'm in a posh bar drinking gin and tonics with the gorgeous model, TV presenter, philanthropist, and bestselling author Katie Piper. It's a tough life. Over the drinks, I learn many remarkable things about my cocktail buddy: the thousands of people she has helped with her charity; her prolific output as a writer, publishing five books in just eight years; her ability to juggle her many work commitments with the demands of being a parent; and the most remarkable thing of all, her approach to life since the day in 2008 when she was raped by her ex-boyfriend and had sulphuric acid thrown in her face.

It was an attack designed to do as much physical harm as possible and in that regard it was horribly successful. After she wakened from an induced twelve-day coma her doctor explained the situation, which in summary was: you're blind in both eyes, you have no face left, you're struggling to breathe because you've swallowed your esophagus, and the police are here to video you in case you don't survive until the trial.

Her immediate response was simple and understandable: *"I just thought to myself, 'I'll do whatever I need to do to get discharged and then quietly go home, take an overdose, and kill myself.'"* The following weeks passed slowly: bedridden, in pain, unable to move, with a nurse present twenty-four hours a day, Katie would silently plan her suicide. But one night when thinking about how to do it, *"something, somewhere said to me: 'Don't kill yourself. I can't tell you why, but there's a bigger reason. You have to stay alive.'"* In that moment, she says, she made what became the most important decision of her life: she chose to be a survivor, not a victim.

That resolve hardened when the time came to be discharged from hospital. She praises the brilliant care she received from the nurses and doctors looking after her, but when people started talking about disability benefits and council flats, she realized just how low expectations were of what her life would become. *"No one said a disfigured woman can still get married, have babies, be sexy, be a CEO, be a trailblazer, be a leader in fashion. So I decided to go out there and reach for everything I wanted. As far as everyone else was concerned I had nothing to lose anyway."*

Part of the recipe of building her new life was acceptance of what had happened. *"I said to myself, I'm never going to look like the old me or Cindy Crawford, but maybe I could be my own kind of beautiful."* Another part was sheer resilience. *"If you look around at all the things that have been achieved, they were usually done by people told there was no hope at all, but they carried on plugging away regardless. I took inspiration from that."* And of course there was a huge degree of bravery, of enduring more than forty operations and skin grafts, of withstanding wearing a mask twenty-three hours a day, of facing the outside world again for the first time. *"In the early days I didn't want to leave the house, I was really agoraphobic, they were dark times. But there came a point where I'd been watching* Loose Women *for a year, wearing pajamas, and I needed to get out."*

As a single woman who aspired to get married and start a family there was also the world of dating to tackle. *"I was living in a one-bed flat in a plastic face mask just trying to get someone to text back, and I thought OK, for all my positivity, this is quite difficult, no one is going to fancy me."* But she wasn't going to let her disability get in the way of what she wanted—to be a mother. *"I started putting money aside to freeze my eggs and started researching how to adopt a child because as far as I was concerned nothing was going to stop me becoming a mum."* In the end she kept going with the dating and did meet a guy, fall in love, get married, and have a child. And there are the glamorous magazine features to prove it.

Katie Piper says people typically just assume disabilities put you at a disadvantage, but she wasn't prepared to accept that. *"People assumed my life was over. I didn't. On paper I should have less opportunities and be unhappy. I should be clinically depressed and dependent on alcohol. But I've never been more positive, and I've never attracted so many positive, successful people into my life."*

Those things people automatically thought would no longer apply to her—getting married, becoming a mom, returning to modeling, running a charity, helping thousands of other burn sufferers—she's done all of them and more. The insight she's gained from these achievements and her experience over these past years inform her best piece of advice:

>*"The whole thing has taught me that the barriers we put before ourselves don't really exist. The only way barriers exist is in our heads. We create them, we feed them, and we choose to keep them alive. So we can also choose to break them down. Confidence and happiness are not luck or something only other people can have, they are decisions you make that involve hard work, commitment, and believing that you actually deserve it. There are no barriers to stop you getting them. And if for whatever reason you ever feel in despair, it is worth remembering God gives his toughest journeys to his strongest soldiers."*

"The only way barriers exist is in our heads. We create them, we feed them, and we choose to keep them alive."

—*Katie Piper*

MICHAEL BLOOMBERG, NEW YORK'S FINEST

O NE OF THE MOST REMARKABLE things about remarkable people is that once they defy the odds by
becoming successful in one area, they often go and
do the same in an entirely different one.

Michael Bloomberg is the quintessential example.

In his thirties, he starts Bloomberg from scratch and grows it
into a global media company, in the process becoming the four-
teenth richest person in the world. That is pretty good going.
Then he sidesteps into politics and becomes the most successful
mayor of all time, presiding over the capital city of the world,
New York City, for an unmatched three terms.

When you meet him in person, it quickly becomes evident
that he is the human manifestation of the city he led. Brusque,
busy, not big on sleep.

He has a reputation for talking fast. And he does. But he is a
man who likes to get things done and get them done early. As
mayor he committed the city to reducing its greenhouse-gas
emissions by 30 percent by 2030, then delivered 19 percent in

just six years. He launched a project to plant a million new trees in New York by 2017: it was completed two years early.

And, like the city, he constantly reinvents himself. He was originally a registered Democrat, then ran for mayor as a Republican, using his own money to fund his campaign so he was beholden to no one. As a Republican, he was pro-choice, pro-gun laws, and pro–immigration reform—all the things, as a Republican, you're not supposed to be. And then when he ran for his third term as New York mayor, which technically, you couldn't even do (but the city council voted to change the rules to allow him), he did so as an Independent, and won.

Then, after this political career, he got busy with philanthropy, giving over $1.8 billion to more than 850 charities. A self-made man with a deep-seated belief in the importance of helping others, funding everything from building new hospitals and furthering education to tackling climate change, including coordinating a nationwide response to the U.S. withdrawal from the Paris climate accord.

In short, the man does not stop.

What's his best advice on how to lead such a full, successful, busy life?

> *"Well, to get anywhere, you've got to work hard, so that means you've got to do something that you love. Who wants a life where you turn up each day to do something you don't like? But most importantly, make sure you actually then get up and do it. There is always someone else who can do what you can do, so you've got to make*

sure you do it first, before the other guy does. You have to get up early every morning and get to it."

In other words, the mayor of the city that never sleeps says, *"Wake up!"*

"There is always someone else who can do what you can do, so you've got to make sure you do it first."

—Michael Bloomberg

ANDY MURRAY,
DROUGHT BREAKER

I S THERE A SPORT TOUGHER to master professionally than tennis? The brutal training schedules that start in childhood and don't stop till you retire; your life constantly on the road, away from family and friends; the very nature of the game itself: a modern-day duel, one person pitted against another, no teammates to share the load; hours of battling, day after day under intense scrutiny; and the mathematically illogical, maddening truth that even though a match can involve over 250 points, each point can prove disproportionately significant. Tennis is arguably the purest, hardest, most unforgiving of all the sports.

Then imagine you have decided to take all that on, decided to shape your life around the sheer unlikeliness of making it as a pro, turned down the tempting football training contract you're offered at an early age, and forgone all other paths through life. Just as your hard work and sacrifices start to pay off and you rise up through the ranks, thanks to a quirk of fate, it turns out that your time coincides with not one but three kings dominating at the highest level, a cartel of tennis

Dons, each showing unprecedented levels of success, skill, and consistency. Knowing that in any other period of time, your own talents and mastery would make you champion many times over, but the universe has served you a dodgy line call just when it counts, what do you do?

If you're Andy Murray, you take it on the chin and do what you have always done: get back to work and keep practicing, keep improving. You get forensic with your technique. Break everything down to the smallest detail, work out how you can get the most from each muscle, each meal, each mind technique. Somehow you absorb and redirect the extraordinary pressure of expectation, channeling that energy into chasing every ball.

And the result? You become the fourth king—starting with Olympic gold, then that first Grand Slam victory at the U.S. Open and then, on the fifth championship point, the most coveted title in tennis, if not all of sports: Wimbledon. The Holy Grail. You become Britain's rainmaker, ending a seventy-seven-year drought for the country. Then three years later, with the British public fragile and fractious from months of bad news, a second Wimbledon victory. You're playing better than ever before, and the world begins to think maybe you're just getting started.

So there is probably no one alive who means and fundamentally inhabits his own words of advice more than Andy Murray:

> *"Always believe that when you apply yourself, you can achieve anything. Make sure you give 100 percent and work as hard as you can in everything you do, not just*

in what you enjoy but also in life. And don't forget, natural ability will only get you so far, there is no substitute for practice."

From the guy who turned practice into perfect.

"Always believe that when you apply yourself, you can achieve anything. . . . Don't forget, natural ability will only get you so far, there is no substitute for practice."

—Andy Murray

DR. MAKI MANDELA'S SHOES

THE FIRST TIME I MEET Dr. Maki Mandela, the eldest surviving child of Nelson Mandela and his wife, Evelyn Mase, is at a charity dinner held in honor of the men who were imprisoned alongside her father. It is an emotional event. The night is to celebrate her father's and his comrades' success in winning freedom for South Africa, but it is tinged with sadness for the price that they, their families, and countless others paid for it. Onstage, Dr. Mandela, resplendently dressed in South African national dress, talks candidly and beautifully about her father, throughout it all remaining strong and serene, a daughter any father would be proud of.

When I meet her later, one on one, it becomes clear that this inner strength and calm extends to not suffering fools gladly. I can tell because I am the fool. I'm a little nervous, and my unclear, rushed introduction is given short shrift: *"So what is it you want to hear from me?"* is her curt response.

I explain I'm interested in her philosophy on life. Fortunately, it is a question that chimes with her.

"With hindsight I've learned that all strength and power comes from within. Over the years I've dealt with my inner demons, my bitterness,

my anger, to look at myself, to take a step to be a better Maki, to live authentically."

The anger she refers to was largely in response to the absence of her father from an early age. *"We had a love-hate relationship. At times I resented the fact that I had lost him to prison."* She talks openly about the reality of her father, the man. *"I know my dad as my dad. I know him with feet of clay. I've seen him in his glory, where he would walk tall, when he would bow to no man, and I've seen him in the last years of his life, when he was sickly and bedridden, and he was dignified until the end. But I know he is flesh and blood; he was like you and me."*

She, of course, still respected him. *"He was very focused. If he said he was going somewhere, it didn't matter what was on that road— he went there. He lived authentically, and true to himself. That's what I admire about my dad."*

Obviously, living in the shadow of a man revered by the world was not easy, something that even Mandela himself acknowledged. *"He always advocated me finding my own path in life. He knew I could not fit in his shoes. He said if your mission is to be the same as your parents, then you have no ambition."*

Her own path was to become a social worker, PhD anthropologist, businesswoman, and vineyard-owning entrepreneur— finding her own way through life, independent of her father's shadow while loving him for who he was. It's reflected in her main piece of advice:

"All the answers that we want are within us. Live your own life. Walk your own path."

—*Dr. Maki Mandela*

SUPER MARIO TESTINO

ARIO TESTINO'S HQ IS EXACTLY what you would hope the home of one of the world's most famous photographers would be like. For a start, the outside of the building is painted as fashionably black as a supermodel's little black dress. Then inside, it's all white and light; big, open studio spaces that cry out for camera equipment and celebrities to turn up so the maestro can do his work. Upon the walls rest shot after shot of some of the world's most famous, beautiful, and talented people, all of whom have stared down Mario's lens and come out looking all the better for it.

In the flesh, Mario is model-handsome himself and understatedly dressed in various shades of navy blue. He is charming to talk to, but if you're prone to feelings of envy, stay away from his Instagram feed. It is an endless stream of photos of fabulous people in wonderful places doing amazing things. And it's not been faked; it's actually what his life consists of. I tell him he seems to be one of the few people whose life is as good as it looks from the outside. He confirms my suspicions. *"I work in a world of the most beautiful people, girls and guys, traveling to the most beautiful places. And I am never anywhere in the world for more than*

five days. I am so lucky. But I really had to pay my dues to get here.
I spent twelve years struggling to get work and start a living, and now
I work a minimum of twelve hours daily."

Mario grew up in a big, loving family in Peru. He was a good
student, and everyone, himself included, assumed he was heading
for a professional career in law or economics. However, when
he hit his teenage years, he *"started to dress weirdly: bright colors,*
stripes, dots, yellow with orange with blue—I couldn't help it; I had to
wear the most outrageous things." His parents, while not understanding it, didn't stop him. But it became clear to all that he
did not fit in with his conservative, Roman Catholic home
country: *"People looked at me like I was a bit of a freak."* He tried
three different university courses, and it didn't work out. After
six months of begging his parents, they sent him to London.

He loved Britain from the beginning. *"I found freedom in*
England—mental freedom, not physical freedom. People here are uptight
with their bodies, but they're free with their minds, they can understand
everything." He felt instinctively that he could be himself. He
applied to and was accepted by a London polytechnic to do
communication studies. The program didn't start till the following
year, so Mario embarked on a course at a local photography
school. Through a friend, Mario was introduced to an Iranian
photographer who had just opened a photography studio, and
Mario was offered a nonpaid job as her assistant. *"In a funny way,*
I learned more there than I did at the photography school, and it taught
me that was what I wanted to do."

From there he said he had no problem getting jobs immediately, but he lost them immediately too. *"I would convince and beg*

people to book me, but I would then light it all wrong and lose the job. It was all on film then, so you couldn't see your mistakes until it was too late." Over time the lessons were learned, he started to keep some jobs and get rebooked for others, and he's been doing *Vogue* shoots for over thirty years now.

He says his enduring success has come down to his insistence on always trying to find the persona of the thing or person he is shooting. *"As a photographer, you have two options: it can either be about you, or it can be about the person you're photographing. I don't do a picture of the Royals thinking of Mario Testino or a picture for Burberry thinking of Mario Testino; I create something for each of them, which captures them."*

Given his global success at doing this, he is unpretentious about his work. *"What people forget is we are salespeople; we make things look good. We can sell you a jacket, a dress, a car, a country, a family, we can sell you anything. We can make you want it."*

He also credits his success to his personal credence of being continually open to change, to movement, to whatever is new. *"I always say I want to be nothing, because then I can be everything, I can be whatever I want to be. Sexuality, taste in food, music, colors, clothes. They all change. I've learned you can never say you like red, because then it's black, then it's yellow, then it's green."*

The biggest lesson he says he's learned from his experiences is therefore to remain malleable, to not resist where life takes you.

"Life is funny. It can be so random, so you have to learn how to sway. You have to be open to what slightly puzzles you, to what you feel curious about, not just what you already like, because then there's no space to grow and become more. In Peru where I grew up, there are earthquakes, and the buildings that are built to sway and move are the ones that usually survive. The ones that are too stiff tend to crack and fall down."

—*Mario Testino*

NO SECRETS WITH CAITLYN JENNER

WHEN YOU WATCH FOOTAGE OF Bruce Jenner winning his gold medal in the men's decathlon at the 1976 Summer Olympics in Montreal, a six-foot-two, lion-maned Adonis, it's not hard to see why he was hailed by the nation as the ultimate All-American Male. What you can't see is the secret contradiction and dark energy that propelled him there—Bruce personally identified as a woman.

I am talking with Caitlyn Jenner, the highest-profile transgender person on the planet. She is reflecting on her previous life as Bruce Jenner and how he came to win that gold medal. *"I look back now, at all the training, the sacrifices, the obsession on timing and technique, and think 'Wow, why would I do that?'"*

The answer is contained within the painful riddle of her life, a riddle finally solved in April 2015 when Bruce became Caitlyn. *"I grew up with gender identity issues. From a young age, I knew there was something not quite right, but this was the 1950s; you were supposed to keep your mouth shut and get on with things, so I tried to push it away and pretend I was a typical guy."*

This inner discombobulation was compounded during Bruce's school years by dyslexia. Not that it was understood as so;

Bruce's struggle to read and write was ascribed to laziness and stupidity.

Both his inner voice and the voices of his elders were telling him there was something wrong with Bruce Jenner. So when it turned out Bruce could run faster than the other kids in gym class, it became the first thing he was congratulated for, and he decided to do more of it. Much more.

What started as an interest in athletics became an obsession. *"It wasn't just about winning, it was about proving to myself I was a worthwhile human being. I wasn't just trying to be best in the team, I was trying to be best in the world. And what better way to prove my masculinity than setting out to become the greatest male athlete on the planet?"*

As smoke screens go, it was literally unbeatable. But the contradiction of being internationally feted for his manhood while he privately identified as a woman was unsustainable, and dark times followed.

The clinical name for the distress Bruce experienced is gender dysphoria, when one's sex and gender don't match one's gender identity. A single chilling statistic shows how extreme that distress can be: over 40 percent of people in the United States who suffer from gender dysphoria attempt suicide, compared to a national average which estimates at less than one percent. At times Bruce considered joining that 40 percent.

He also considered coming out. Tired of living the ultimate lie, Bruce began plastic surgery procedures in the early 1980s to make his features look more feminine, but the fear of the publicity and the overwhelming sense of shame he felt stopped him.

So he buried his secret again and continued to present as a man, secretly wearing women's underwear beneath his suit, a hidden homage to who he was on the inside.

That denial of self, and the battle to fill the expectations placed upon him by society, affected every aspect of Bruce's life, fracturing marriages and relationships, sideswiping his career, and fostering addictions. *"When you suffer from gender identity issues, it is always there. You can't just take two aspirins and get over it."*

The turning point came when he found himself single in his early 60s. *"Here I was, after all my kids were raised, in a house by myself dealing with the same internal issues as ten years ago, and I thought to myself, 'What am I going to do? I can't take this anymore.'"* So after years of soul searching, he confronted his fears, consulted his God (his pastor helped Bruce reach a conclusion that transitioning as a person in the public eye could be the reason why he was put on this planet), and decided to retire Bruce and give birth to Caitlyn, aged sixty-four.

What strikes me about the woman I am talking to about this previous life is the graceful, gentle, and open way she recounts it. There is a generosity and lack of bitterness towards the media who hounded her and the people who vilified her, saying no more than, *"The internet can be horrible."* I point this peacefulness out to her and she replies quietly and profoundly, *"My soul is better than it's ever been. I now don't have any secrets and that is a wonderful thing."* She talks repeatedly about how supportive her family was, with one of her sons simply telling Caitlyn that he had never been more proud.

Caitlyn sees part of her role now as promoting awareness of gender dysphoria and the silent torture people can experience from it. She knows the pain of keeping things hidden, but now also knows the joy and release that can come from getting things out into the open. Bruce may have been a person in conflict, but Caitlyn is someone at peace.

Her life story and mission directly inform her best piece of advice:

> *"The bottom line is there is nothing better than going through life with no secrets. So be open about who you are as a person. Wake up in the morning and be yourself. Live your life unashamed of who you are and without the burden of secrets."*

And there can be no better ambassador for that approach than Caitlyn Jenner.

"Live your life unashamed of who you are and without the burden of secrets."

—*Caitlyn Jenner*

ANTHONY BOURDAIN:
LEAN, MEAN GRILLING MACHINE

I F YOU'VE EVER READ *Kitchen Confidential*, the restaurant petticoat–lifting book by Anthony Bourdain, bad–boy chef, writer, and TV presenter, you'll already know his advice to never order fish on a Tuesday. Here are some additional pearls of wisdom that he gave me recently, in his words. All I'll say is I'm very glad I got to our appointment early.

1. Turn the f**k up on time.
"I am punctual—that's probably the most useful lesson I ever learned. It is the first evidence of your character I have: are you the sort of person who says they're going to do something and then doesn't? Being on time is the first thing I require of my cooks. If you have problems doing that, chances are I'm wasting my time showing you how to make hollandaise sauce. It's the same in social relationships—do you have enough respect for me to show up on time, or do you not? If you don't, we're probably going to have problems down the line."

2. Working in a kitchen will straighten you out.
"I was a spoiled, narcissistic, lazy, self-involved middle-class kid from

the suburbs. *I'm a person who, left to my own natural instincts, will gravitate toward chaos and self-destruction and addiction. But working in a kitchen forced upon me a discipline that stopped me from spinning out. I started as a dishwasher at seventeen, and it may have taken thirty years, but I learned how to grow up and be an adult there.*"

3. Be polite to waiters.

"*If you're mean or dismissive to waiters and hotel staff, you're dead to me, or if not dead to me, you are bleeding out—our time together is going to be very limited. Because if you're pissy to waiters, that's the real you: you may not be like that to me now, but you will be.*"

4. Don't work with assholes.

"*If you don't like the people you work with, you'll end up fucking miserable. Any accrued benefits are kind of worthless because your life will be shit. If you're dealing with assholes the whole time, you'll die of a heart attack. You know the people I'm talking about—the ones that when you see their caller ID you think, 'Oh fuck, I don't want to talk to them.' Well, don't do business with those people. Mikey Corleone said it isn't personal, it's business. Bullshit: all business is personal.*"

5. When you're a cook, you can't bullshit anyone.

"*The kitchen is a world of absolutes: you either can or cannot cook 300 eggs Benedict in a three-hour shift. You might talk about how great you are all the time, but we're going to find out. Whatever you say before or afterward is meaningless. But if you're really good, they'll bump you up. It's like the Mafia: if you kill eight people, you get to be a made guy.*"

6. If you get a lucky break, work it.

"If you're forty-four years old like I was, and you've fucked up your life in every way like I had, make sure you recognize a lucky break when you get one, like I did with my book. Then work really hard at not fucking it up, because that's what most people do when they get lucky. I managed to avoid that. I didn't have a plan—I just worked hard, avoided assholes, and always turned up on time."

7. Don't be a dick.

"If I'm at your house and you offer me something to eat I don't particularly like, I'm going to smile and eat it. Try to be a good guest, try to be grateful, be a good guy, don't be a dick."

8. Avoid hippies.

"Hippies. I hate hippies and I hate their music. Bad for morale, bad work habits. And they are never on time."

As I say, I'm glad I turned up early.

"If you're forty-four years old like I was, and you've fucked up your life in every way like I had, make sure you recognize a lucky break when you get one, like I did with my book. Then work really hard at not fucking it up, because that's what most people do when they get lucky. I managed to avoid that. I didn't have a plan—I just worked hard, avoided assholes, and always turned up on time."

—*Anthony Bourdain*

DOING TIME WITH
ALEXANDER McLEAN

O
UR DRIVER PARKS ALONGSIDE A group of mud huts
scattered around a clearing of baked, dry earth, turns
off the ignition, and announces that we're here. I
say this can't be the right place; there aren't any walls or
fences. *"Why would there be fences?"* replies the driver, *confused by
my comment. "There isn't anywhere for the prisoners to escape to."*

I'm having my expectations of what it is to be incarcerated
in Africa blown apart by a ten-jail tour of Uganda and Kenya
with Alexander McLean, the founder of the African Prisons
Project (APP). This is our first stop, a prison farm, officially in
the middle of nowhere among the vast prairie lands of rural
northern Uganda. It's taken five hours of driving on unpaved
roads to get here. But still, no fences at all?

Alexander explains that not only are walls unnecessary but the
local community prefers it this way because then they can use
the prison well. That's when I see the prison's water pump,
and the orderly line in front of it, consisting not just of inmates
but young schoolchildren too, both groups in their respective
uniforms, happily waiting their turn to draw from the well; a
scene unimaginable in the Western world.

Later, as we walk around the grounds, a prisoner comes bounding up to us. He is speaking in a local dialect that I can't understand, but one thing is clear: he is very excited to see Alexander. The prison officer with us translates: *"He says that Alexander McLean saved his life. Alexander visited the prisoner on death row and helped him mount an appeal. When the date came, Alexander swapped his suit, shirt, and tie for the prisoner's rags so he would look smart before the judge. The appeal worked, and the prisoner will be a free man in a matter of days."*

I turn to Alexander to verify the story, and in his grave and modest manner he nods and says it is true. I ask him, out of interest, did he get his suit back? *"I don't believe I did. I am sure he will return it one day"* is his measured, if somewhat optimistic, reply.

This small exchange captures both the essence of APP's work and Alexander's unconditional commitment to it. APP goes into prisons where there are little or no medical, educational, or legal facilities and doesn't leave until there are health centers, libraries, teachers, and lawyers in place. They've reduced mortality rates by a factor of ten in some jails, coached illiterate inmates through all stages of education (in some cases, prisoners have obtained law degrees and now help other inmates), and have gotten countless death sentences overturned. Game-changing doesn't cover it. Alexander is a founder and leader so committed to the mission that he's even prepared to literally lose the shirt off his back.

In fact, that's not even the best example of how all-in Alexander is with regard to his work; that story comes when we visit a maximum-security prison closer to town. The conditions are beyond challenging. I spend time in an open cell with 280 men who have to alternate sleeping and sitting because there is not enough room for all of them to lie down at the same time. Even tougher than that is the TB "ward"—a bare, dark concrete room given over to quarantining those men with the contagious disease. While my friend and I stay back at the doorway, concerned for our health, Alexander walks straight in and over to the man who appears to be in the worst health. He gets down on his hands and knees, and with a small cloth starts to mop the man's brow and tend to him. Without being overly dramatic, I think to myself, that is exactly what Jesus would do.

Alexander is a religious man. He first visited Africa as an eighteen-year-old when he volunteered at a hospice in Uganda. It was when working in the hospital he noticed that prisoners brought in were often left chained to the bed and not given treatment. He couldn't help thinking if they were treated this badly in the hospital, how much worse was it in prison? So he talked his way into one and found out. So appalling were the conditions, he found himself compelled to raise money to build a basic health center and library. His work reduced the mortality rate from 144 to 12 in one year, and he hasn't stopped doing such work since.

Alexander points out that most people in these prisons are there for crimes of poverty: stealing food, not paying debts, being a vagabond (the Dickensian-sounding "crime" of being homeless). Most have not even been to trial; they are just held on remand. The Ugandan constitution says that no one should wait more than six months for their day in court, yet the current average is two and a half years. The result: prisons are hugely over-crowded with, more often than not, innocent people. It's a depressing situation.

Alexander's work brings hope to such places. He of course makes no distinctions between whether people are innocent or not: he starts from the position that they are all human beings and deserve to be able to live and, inevitably sometimes, die with dignity. But more than that, he is motivated to tackle the lost opportunity of keeping people in captivity with no chance for change. He wants whatever time people have to spend in prison to be an opportunity for transformation, not despair. And on this trip, I meet enough ex–death row prisoners who became lawyers assisting their fellow inmates, as well as recently trained prisoner-teachers leading English classes for other convicts, to know that such transformations are possible.

He is a truly remarkable man, shining light into some of the darkest places imaginable. His life is a manifestation of the advice he gives:

> *"The lowliest-looking person is filled with gifts and talents beyond your imagination. Love such people as yourself. Those living on the margins of society do not need to have their problems solved for them; they just need to be given the opportunities to solve them themselves. And in doing so, they will often also solve the problems of others."*

"The lowliest-looking person is filled with gifts and talents beyond your imagination. Love such people as yourself."

—*Alexander McLean*

BREAKFAST WITH BILL GATES
BY EDWARD DOCX

THE EMAIL FROM RICHARD DROPS into my inbox on Monday at 8:47 A.M. Can I go and have breakfast with Bill Gates and get his best piece of advice? I am in a rush as usual but there's no way I'm going to pass up such a request, so I put "breakfast with Bill Gates" in my calendar for Thursday morning without a second thought.

I've known Richard for twenty-five years and he's one of my closest friends. I would do anything he asked, no matter how improbable. He would do anything I asked, no matter how improbable. I know this because we're constantly asking each other to do improbable things and then . . . well, doing them. Our shared motto is *"there's always a way"* and we have an unspoken understanding that we'll never let each other down. He's asked me to interview Bill Gates because he's going to the Grand Canyon with his dad. This is definitely one of his better requests.

Thursday arrives. I get up at 6:00 A.M. I have an unforeseen hangover. I check my calendar. . . . It's bad.

Today is the last day of the tense negotiations to sell my family home. (I have not found us somewhere else to live, which the rest of the family feel strongly is an issue.) Also, today is publication day of my new novel, the first in four years, on which a hell of a lot rides: money, career, sanity. I am therefore due on the radio in an hour or so to talk about fathers and sons, a theme of the book. Additionally, I am late on two unnecessarily complicated pieces of journalism and am expected at a couple of bookstore signings before noon. At lunchtime I'm being interviewed by a newspaper, about my mother turning out to be Russian. Further, I have a political assignment due by the end of the day. Right now, though, I have four children whom I must feed, dress, and take to school and . . . Oh, Christ—no! I have totally forgotten that today I am *having breakfast with Bill Gates*.

My wife is already leaving for work. I think she said in Lisbon, if I heard her right, but it's simply too embarrassing not to know this. So I nod. She casually recites from memory a to-do list for the next two days, none of which I process. Then she asks what my plans are for the day. I'm seeing Bill Gates, I say, for breakfast. Computer guy. Richest man in the world. She frowns indulgently. She thinks I am a fantasist. Great. Who's taking the children in, she asks? Matthew, our neighbor, I say. I am a fantasist because in my calendar it says that *I* am taking in *his* children. Have fun, she says. See you Saturday. . . . Deep breath. It's all do-able. I'm just going to have to drop the kids at school ninety minutes early—that will surprise everyone—and then leave the car in a nearby supermarket to save traffic-time on the way back and then take a bus, subway, cab, somehow. . . .

Outwardly serene but inwardly levitational with anxiety, I arrive ten minutes late for breakfast with Bill Gates. But the first thing that hits me is that my being late for Bill Gates doesn't matter. Why? Because they are neither waiting for me nor expecting me. Why? Because there are two hundred other people here; maybe two hundred fifty. This is not the intimate breakfast I had anticipated. I try to find Richard's email. Somehow I have deleted it. My phone is my enemy.

And now it starts pinging. It's the realtor. The buyer is dropping his price. What do I want to do? Urgent.

Obviously, Richard has not concentrated on the emails any more than I have. His tone (as far as I can recall) had suggested a cozy breakfast. Perhaps Bill and I exchange ideas with regard to the future of humanity. I take notes; Bill takes notes; a few deferential middle men nod along; that kind of thing. But this is not what we're looking at here. No, this is several hundred heavyweight business and political leaders talking global strategy and purposefully sipping fruit smoothies amidst the oligarch-chic of the Four Seasons Hotel.

My phone pings again. Can I go on the radio earlier? I wince and delay responding. This, I realize, is my own business strategy.

Not to worry. All I have to do is track down David, the organizer. Richard will have briefed him. So I find someone who finds someone who finds someone who can take me to David. And there he is . . . with Bill. Bill Gates.

David looks like a man under stress who is an expert at appearing like he's not a man under stress. I empathize. He's organized this breakfast and invited everyone significant in the First World—for him, as host, this must be a harrowing few hours: everything has to go right. You and me both, buddy, you and me both. The woman I'm with doesn't want to interrupt him. We hover anxiously, pretending not to be anxious, or hovering. There's a moment like a gap in the traffic that nobody thinks you're going to shoot for. She shoots for it. My kind of girl.

"Hello, David." I smile. "I'm Ed."

"Ed?" He twists momentarily from Bill Gates, grand-wizard of human modernity, world-changing philanthropist, the richest man on the planet, education powerhouse, and saver of millions of lives.

"I'm here to do Richard's thing."

David's face is unequivocally blank.

"Richard's thing," I say, eloquently. "One important thing. I mean, if you had to say one thing. To someone. Else."

There's a flicker of not quite annoyance but dude-I-am-so-busy-right-now-and-all-these-people-are-waiting-and-this-is-Bill-Gates-and-he's-here-for-me-and-what-the-hell-are-you-talking-about?

"One piece of advice."

"Oh," he says. "Okay, right."

I feel like *David's* one piece of advice for me right now might be a slightly stronger version of "go away," but we're both saved from that by someone ushering him to usher Bill into the breakfast room.

Inside the intimate breakfast room, there are roughly twenty tables with a dozen or so people at each. I feel like I'm seated at the one furthest away from Bill as possible. I'm next to someone who runs a bank that runs banks and a colossus of a man from Russia whose card says he is a masseur and a medium. I need to get back to David somehow. But he's sitting down near Bill and breakfast has started and they're probably already talking about the future of humanity. I feel a pulse of deeper apprehension. But I'm not going to let Richard down. It's still all doable.

During breakfast, I surreptitiously respond to dozens of emails while talking amicably about tarot and collapsing currency. Texts arrive. My phone is backing up on voice mails. The school: can they be clear that parents are not allowed to leave children with security in the morning before Early Club starts? My wife at the airport: why are the buyers dropping the price? *The Sunday Times:* let's talk about the family piece! It's probably still all doable. To buy time, I hit on a simple holding formula and start responding with the same line that I can copy and paste to everyone: "Having breakfast with Bill Gates. Back to you shortly."

Now we're into Bill's talk. There will be questions afterwards. Great, I can ask the big one then. Bill is fascinating.

Questions. Hands go up. Mine first. David has the roving mike. (Hello, David, over here, over here . . .) But it's the Very Important Politicians who seem to be invited ahead of me. I start straining, like a child at school who is desperate to impress the teacher. I have to get in. Have to. I catch David's eye. He's passing me to get the mike to some CEO. Not so fast, dude, not so fast. I manage to catch him. He has the demeanor of someone dealing with a drunk at the back of a church.

I whisper, "Shall I ask my question now or after?"

"After," he says, confidentially. "At the end."

Breakthrough! He knows. He has remembered. And he's going to sort it. Finally.

The formal questions end. I get up. I'm ready to meet Bill. But . . . WTF?

Bill is *leaving*. That's what. And he's leaving really fast. Richest-man-in-the-world fast. He's three deep in security, being whisked away towards a side door. Has David forgotten his promise? No way! This does not happen. Not on my watch.

All of a sudden, I'm barrelling across the room like an action movie hero, hell bent on rescuing his pal. There's no way Bill Gates is leaving without speaking to me. No way. Me and Rich, we never . . . But . . .

He's at the side exit door. If he leaves, I know with a sudden cold and terrifying certainty that I'll never see him again. But I'm all distilled purpose now. I'm pure focus. They can't stop me. I'm coming through. Coming through.

I'm almost there when . . . Bam!

Security. I'm blocked. They're *afraid* of me. No, no, no, no, no, no. I'm not a terrorist, bro, I am . . . I'm a novelist. It's totally different. Too late. Bill has gone.

But, wait, there's another door. I'm through it. I'm in a corridor. Running. I can see him. Ten steps behind. Hang on, Mr. Gates, hang on! Richard, don't worry. This is not *not* happening. Here I come, Bill. I'm closing, I'm closing . . .

Gates peels off. I peel the same way. He's going into the men's room. This is it. This is my chance. I'm good with people in bathrooms. I put people at their ease in bathrooms. If I have to pop the question over the urinals, or under the cubicle door, then so be it. So be it.

Blocked again! Big, tall, serious, security. Never been more serious. No way am I getting into that toilet, he says.

"But I really need to pee here, buddy!"

Security is implacable, they're not buying my wee story. Okay, I'll wait. I'll wait. I'll . . . Wait! Bill's coming out.

I move so fast that the security cameras must have me as a blur.

"Hello, Mr. Gates," I say. "I'm writing a book in which I ask people like you if they had one piece of advice that . . . Well, I'm not writing it. My friend Richard is. You know, the just one thing book? Richard? David? Did he? Did they? Okay, no . . . But anyway Richard can't be here today. He's with his dad. I think they're in the Grand Canyon. Doesn't matter. So, anyway, yes, I'm a novelist. I write books and screenplays and . . ." We're walking side by side towards the elevator. Oddly I can feel he is tolerating me. I can't be certain but I think it's the novelist line that's holding him. "And I'm really interested in your answer. If you were talking to . . . If you had one piece of advice for a young man or woman . . ." His security has to indulge me—because Bill Gates is listening.

"Mr. Gates, if you had one piece of advice to share with your fellow *Homo sapiens* about life—one thing you'd like to pass on—what would that be?"

Bill Gates stands still. Bill Gates, cofounder of Microsoft, the world's greatest philanthropist, and global visionary *sine qua non,* stands dead still and considers the question with his full concentration. Our eyes meet. Everyone around us is leaning in. We all want to know.

And then Bill Gates says something so surprising . . . and so personally gratifying . . . and so unexpected . . . that I have to fight the urge to kiss him.

"If there's just one piece of advice I could give, then I would urge people to foster a love of reading. It's our core skill as human beings. It's the gateway to everything else. It gets you involved. It allows your curiosity to follow its course. It connects us across time and space. Books and reading are the most important things. Yes, I would say above all else, I would urge people to foster a love of reading. Start as early as you can and keep on reading."

There's a moment. Human to human. He smiles at me. I smile at him.

"Thank you," I say.

Then security envelopes him and he's gone. And then I remember: I am publishing my book today. I stand on my own in the hallway and I feel happier than I have felt in a long time. There's a message on my screen that says simply: "Happy Publication Day."

"I would urge people to foster a love of reading. Start as early as you can and keep on reading."

—*Bill Gates*

THE ESSENCE OF JO MALONE

I T'S THE WEATHER OF UNICORNS—a sunny day in London—
so we order rosé wine to celebrate. A selection is available,
and the different wines are presented to sample. Jo Malone
lifts each glass to try. I assume she's going to taste them, but she
chooses simply by smelling each one. I think to myself afterward,
of course she does.

Jo Malone is one of the most famous fragrance-makers in the
world. As the founder of not one but now two internationally
successful perfume businesses, Jo Malone is a name most people
know but few know her story. If she were to capture the essence
of it in just three words, it would be this: *"lemonade from lemons."*

Jo is a self-described dyslexic working-class girl from Bexleyheath
who's done good. She may have a natural-born talent for creating
fragrances, which she partly credits to her dyslexia—*"My brain
just works differently; I see textures and colors and can translate them
back into smells and fragrances"*—but her first foray into beauty
products was for traumatic reasons. When Jo was eleven, her mum
had a serious nervous breakdown, and social services said if her
mother was hospitalized, Jo and her sister would have to go
into care.

Amazingly, Jo convinced the social worker that she could handle the responsibility of providing for the family. To earn money, she recalled what she'd seen her mom do as a Revlon lady: make face creams at home and sell them to well-to-do ladies in Fulham. So she did that. It worked, making her enough money to look after the family until her mom recovered. *"I learned early that when bad things happen, you can either let them beat you or you can stand and fight. And if you do, you can always turn things round."*

A second, earlier childhood experience proved equally formative: the time Jo was made to stand on a desk by a teacher as punishment for sneaking a look at a friend's exam paper. (Jo's dyslexia meant she did not understand one of the written questions.) *"I felt so utterly humiliated. And she said in front of the whole class that if you cheat, you will never make anything of your life, Jo Malone."*

When Jo recounts this story, you can still feel the emotional charge, even though it is nearly forty years later. *"I've remembered that moment all through my life. I've never allowed it to make me bitter, but I have allowed it to motivate me. I remember looking out of the window of our little house and thinking, 'She's wrong. I'm going to make something of my life, I'm not going to stay here.'"*

Of course, her childhood didn't consist of just these negative moments. She has fond memories of her dad: *"He was a brilliant human being but didn't know how to hold a family together."* His life instead revolved around three things, all of which came to be instrumental in Jo's success: he was an artist, a market-trader, and a magician, and Jo worked alongside him on all three. *"Saturday mornings, I would work with him on the market, helping him sell his paintings, and in the evenings I was his magician's assistant. I had a pet white dove called Suki that my dad would make appear out of a pan of fire."* Collectively, these experiences schooled her in the tricks of the retailing trade, teaching her how to use stories and a bit of magic to captivate people, all crucial ingredients in the kaleidoscopic world of senses and surprises that she has created.

This blend of different experiences, both good and bad, have all contributed to Jo's life view. *"Looking back, everything was relevant. Nothing in life is wasted. You can make something positive from anything."*

Being diagnosed with breast cancer in her mid-thirties was the ultimate test of this approach to life. She was dressed in her best suit and earrings on her way to a glamorous summer party when she got the news. Her doctor said it was one of the worst forms of aggressive breast cancer he'd seen, and she had nine months left to live. Her instinct to fight did not kick in immediately. That came a bit later, as she sat on her bed crying, with her two-year-old son asking his mommy what the matter was.

"At the thought of leaving him, the spirit to fight just filled me. I thought to myself, 'No one's going to tell me when I'm going to die. I'll tell you when I'm going to die.'"

She credits her husband with a powerful piece of advice. *"He told me to fight the cancer in the same way I built my business, and that stuck in my mind. I knew that if I were in trouble in business, I would find the best lawyer. So I went to find the best doctor."* Three days later, Jo was on a plane to the U.S. She put herself in the care of a cutting-edge oncologist and endured chemotherapy every five days for a year, an unbelievably grueling twelve months, but she was ultimately delivered the all-clear. *"On my last day of chemo, I dressed in the same suit and earrings I was meant to go to that party in, and I took back that day that the cancer took from me."*

While beating cancer is clearly the biggest obstacle she has had to overcome, Jo talks about selling her business as being traumatic too. Not only did she suffer that sense of loss entrepreneurs often feel when they exit their company, she also lost the right to use her own name in business in the future, as that was now owned by the new company, and she no longer got to do the thing she loved most in the world: make fragrances. So what did she do? As soon as her non-compete contract ended, she started building her second empire, Jo Loves, one scent and one shop at a time.

Her advice reflects this lifelong spirit of defiance and refusal to be dictated to by external circumstances. She counsels that we should remember that, ultimately, we are always in control.

> **"No matter how bad it is, no situation is ever greater than you. You always have three options: you can change the situation, accept the situation, or change your mind-set on how you see the situation. And you have the power in your hands to choose whichever is best for you. Never allow something else or someone's opinion to become the title of your book. Ever."**

She says the last part with such verve and passion, it's clear that if you could take what Jo's got and bottle it, you'd make a lot of money.

"I learned early that when bad things happen, you can either let them beat you or you can stand and fight. And if you do, you can always turn things round."

—*Jo Malone*

BEAR GRYLLS, BORN SURVIVOR

YOU COULD BE FORGIVEN FOR assuming that Bear Grylls, ex-soldier, Everest climber, world-renowned survival expert and adventurer, would be a bit macho, hardened by his time as a soldier and his many brushes with death—but it's not so. I wouldn't be so stupid as to call Bear a bit of a softy, especially when sitting right in front of him, but he has a warmth and a gentleness you don't necessarily expect of your typical SAS commando.

We're chatting backstage after Bear has just talked to hundreds of teachers about tackling Everest at a young age (he reached the summit at twenty-three, two years after a sky-diving accident in which he fractured his spine and was told he may never walk again) and the source of his drive and resilience. Interestingly, when you hear him recount his adventures, there's no bravado: achievements are downplayed, credit for them is assigned to others, and he portrays himself as someone who constantly struggles along the way.

In Bear's world, struggling is OK. In fact, it is enduring the struggle that leads to the success.

"There's always going to be someone faster, smarter, taller, more experienced than you, but the rewards in life don't always go to them; the rewards in life go to the dogged, the determined, those who can keep going and pick themselves back up and never say die and just hang in there, sometimes quietly and undramatically."

One on one, his humbleness remains and, while not shy, he comes across as someone more comfortable heading up a mountain than to a cocktail party. First and foremost, he's a family man. Much of what he says relates back either to his parents or his experience of being a parent himself. His introduction to the world of adventure came from his dad, who took him climbing when he was young. Bear loved the bonding experience, with his father quite literally showing him the ropes. *"It was the first time I found something I was good at. I never did well at school, but I could climb higher than anyone else."* It opened him up to a life of *"being outdoors, going on adventures, getting muddy and doing a job I couldn't even have dreamed of back as a young boy."*

As with most people who have a career that professionalizes a relationship with danger, he's extremely respectful of the risks he takes. He makes it clear that he didn't "conquer" Everest: *"We didn't conquer anything; we made it to the top by the skin of our teeth and got away with our lives, where others hadn't."* Four people he knew died on the mountain at the same time Bear was climbing it.

He lightens the mood by recounting the time he proudly showed his mom the photo of himself at the summit of Everest, a picture taken after a grueling three-month expedition, with days spent in the death zone gasping for air, knowing each footstep could be his last. She took one look at the shot and said, *"Oh, Bear, it would have been so much nicer if you could have just combed your hair."*

"Mums will be mums," he says, smiling at the memory.

He credits part of his ability to endure the hardships of his adventuring to his faith. While he points out *"there are no atheists in the death zone,"* his quiet Christianity is something he calls upon away from the mountains on a daily basis. *"I know I can't depend just on self-confidence—by myself, I am not strong enough—but developing a confidence in something much stronger than me gives me more power, so I start every day on my knees just quietly asking for help and wisdom and to say sorry for the things I got wrong yesterday."*

He's non-evangelical about his faith but open about it and, it has to be said, gives God some great PR opportunities. One of his all-time heroes, President Obama, came on his *Running Wild* show to raise awareness of climate change (and he schooled Mr. President on the dangers of fornicating bears and the benefits of drinking urine). He also asked if he could pray with the President, who, as another man of faith and family values, readily agreed.

Given his approach to faith, family, and friendships, it's surprising that Bear is sometimes the target of criticism for his TV shows, which some claim promote machismo and the spilling of blood and sweat and tears. He has no time for that negativity, and says anyone who thinks that's the takeaway from his programs is missing the point. In fact, he says what his TV programs show, time and time again, is what he also puts forward as his best piece of advice:

"It is not the most masculine, macho, or the ones with the biggest muscles who win. It's those who look after each other, who remain cheerful in adversity, who are kind and persistent and positive. These are the characteristics that help you, not just to survive life but to enjoy it. And they're nothing to do with gender. The people who are successful are the ordinary ones that just go that little bit further, who give a little more than they are asked to, who live within that extra 5 percent."

—Bear Grylls

THE EDUCATION OF DAMBISA MOYO

I F YOU EVER WANT A role model for the transformational power of education and the unlimited potential of Africa, you will struggle to find a better candidate than the global economist and bestselling author Dambisa Moyo. Born and raised in post-colonial Zambia, forty years later she's sitting before me as an Oxford PhD– and Harvard MBA–wielding, Barclays board–sitting, razor-sharp woman who was ranked among the 100 Most Influential People in the World by *Time* magazine—with enough energy to power her home continent.

She is crystal clear on how she made the journey from her origins to the life she leads now. *"The linchpin of my life was being able to go to school."* She sets this in context: *"Look, I've got no birth certificate, because at the time of my birth, birth certificates were not issued to blacks, so you can imagine there wasn't much emphasis on girls like me going to school."* But her parents were different. Even though they had been born into a country where there were restrictions on blacks going to school, they knew the importance of Dambisa getting an education. *"They said, 'You have to go to school—we don't know what that might look like for you, but you've got to go and do that.' And that changed the trajectory of my life forever."*

Her African schooling is something she is grateful for and why she rallies against, and works to overturn, the lazy misconceptions of Africa as a hopeless cause, eternally dependent on aid. *"Along side the Caribbean Islands, my continent produces over 90 percent of the blacks that go to the Ivy League universities in the United States. Africa is viewed as the continent of corruption and disease, poverty and war, but it's the source of the vast majority of blacks that go to those schools and can compete globally. As a child, I was better educated in Africa than many people I know who grew up in the West."*

She fears that these same Western societies are becoming inadvertently racially disconnected, where blacks and whites live in the same cities but with increasingly separate lives. *"I just came from a business lunch in Mayfair. There were sixty people there. I was the only black person and the only woman. I knew people there, and I would go to the gallows saying they are not racist. But I looked around and thought 'Wow . . . this is London and, if I weren't here, there wouldn't be a single black person or woman in this room.'"*

She is also clear about saying that direct forms of prejudice are still alive and well in the twenty-first century. She tells the quietly shocking story of attending her first public AGM/shareholders' meeting of a large global company as their newly appointed director. While sitting onstage with her board colleagues—all of whom were white and male—a question came from the floor from a woman who asked crossly, *"I want to know what credentials that woman has to allow her to be on the board."* When the chairman explained that all his board members were of the highest caliber, the lady grew agitated, saying you have to answer my question, what are her credentials. A colleague was quick to point out, *"She has a doctorate in economics from Oxford and a master's from Harvard, and she worked for ten years at Goldman Sachs. Is there anything else you want to say?"*

I asked Dambisa if the assumption that she doesn't deserve to be there rails her in some way. *"It's what you deal with every single day being a minority. You learn to not respond to it and to not let it define you. So I just sat there and thought, 'Look, lady, I'm fine, you don't need to worry about me and my credentials.' And here's the thing, when I walked off the podium, two of the male board members said to me, 'Thank God they didn't ask about my credentials,' including one who said he hadn't even been to college."*

When it comes to her most valuable advice, it is these decades of confounding expectations and enduring ignorant assumptions about Africa, about women, about her color that serve as the backdrop to a deeper, more fundamental piece of guidance:

> *"I know it sounds kind of corny, but every day I look in the mirror and I tell myself that I am going to go out there and face it and not curl up in a ball because somebody said something or thinks that I couldn't be or do something simply because of who I am. It's hard, but you have to do it. Put in the hard work, discipline and focus and just keep going. Remember there are numerous people, both similar and dissimilar to you, who are rooting for you to stay strong, and to prove the naysayers wrong."*

THE BEAT OF MICKEY HART

REMARKABLE PEOPLE TEND TO BE focused; it goes with the territory. But no one, and I do mean no one, is more focused than Mickey Hart, drummer of the Grateful Dead, the seminal psychedelic rock band from the 1960s to the present day. Mickey's "thing" is rhythm. And he is all in.

On the occasion when our paths first cross, I hear him before I see him. There's a beat—a knocking, tocking sound—and a haunting wail coming from a secluded, fire-lit corner in this remote part of the Guatemalan Highlands where we're staying.

Intrigued, I move toward the beat and find Mickey, cross-legged on the floor, eyes closed, gently swaying in front of the fire, with four Mayan shamans blowing, shaking, and hitting their traditional ceremonial instruments, the same ancient rhythms and noises the Mayans have been making among these rain forest–clad hills for millennia. And Mickey is feeling it.

He has flown into this far-flung spot to jam with the shamans in his never-ending search for new sounds and beats. This is what he does. He does rhythm.

To put it into context, this is a man who has a specially built lab at home in which he sits wearing his own specially built rhythm helmet, a device wired up to an MRI scanner to measure the effect on his brain of the different beats he plays. This is the same man who has worked with NASA to listen to the rhythm of the universe, recording the distant beats and rumbles from remote galaxies, describing the Big Bang as *"the first note, the downbeat of the universe."* It's all pretty cosmic, in every sense of the word, but these are serious endeavors. His latest project has him working with doctors on a study of the effect of different rhythms on disease: are there certain frequencies that can affect unhealthy cells and help them? If anyone can find out, it's Mickey.

His advice, therefore, came as no surprise.

> *"If I was to give one piece of advice, it is this: life is all about rhythm. Your heartbeat, great sex, the seasons, how often you call your parents, your good days versus your bad days, your DNA, the universe, everything has a rhythm. You have to develop a well-stretched ear and listen. The more you listen for the rhythm of your life, the more you will hear it. Find your rhythm. Live your life to its beat."*

But for now he is back with the shamans. They're still playing in their trancelike state, summoning past ancestors, gods, and monsters. Mickey is reverential to the shamans and respectful of their traditions, but he's also a perfectionist. To his ear, something's not quite right, something's a little off. It's the conch shell. Or more specifically, it is the way the conch shell is being blown.

Mickey knows a better way. He stops the proceedings, explains via the translator the nature of the issue, and in one short blast Mickey improves on 5,000 years of technique. The shamans look impressed.

"Find your rhythm. Live your life to its beat."

—Mickey Hart

NANCY HOLLANDER,
JIU-JITSU LAWYER

I'M DRINKING PEPPERMINT TEA WITH David, Goliath's nemesis. But David is not how I expected him to be. First, he is a woman. Secondly, she's American. And finally, she's petite and in her seventies.

You probably haven't heard of Nancy Hollander, which is a good thing for you personally. As an American criminal defense and civil rights attorney, she'd only come across your radar if you were, rightly or wrongly, in trouble. But without her, there is a dark part of the world we would know a lot less about: Guantánamo Bay.

Nancy Hollander is the lawyer for two of the men incarcerated in that prison, set up on foreign land by the U.S. government under the George W. Bush administration. It was seemingly the deliberate aim not just to imprison men they suspected of terrorist activity, but to do so indefinitely, unaccountably, with no charge but with plenty of torture, and in direct contravention of constitutional and human rights. However, if Nancy knows one thing, it's that the law is bigger than the government. So she is many years into a legal fight on behalf of her clients to get the U.S.

government to abide by its own laws. It is a painfully slow battle, but one she is starting to win.

As a master strategist, she engineered a tactical success by winning the right for one of her clients, Mohamedou Ould Slahi, to publish *Guantánamo Diary,* a memoir recounting the extraordinary rendition, dark sites, savage beatings, torture, and sexual humiliation he has experienced during his fourteen years in captivity. It made for uncomfortable reading, especially for the American government. The furor around the book helped to bring attention not only to the abuses, but also to the reality of Mohamedou's situation, that he had been held in Guantánamo Bay for well over a decade, not charged with any crime, and even after the former chief prosecutor in Guantánamo had said publicly that there was no evidence that Mohamedou had ever committed any violence against the United States.

His case, or lack of one, has been a troubling manifestation of the illegal practices that Nancy constantly fights.

But she has fought successfully. After more than a decade, Nancy finally obtained approval for Mohamedou's release. Her work continues.

In conversation, Nancy is absolutely focused on due process. She will not reveal a single piece of potentially classified information about any of her clients or the conditions in which they are held, even if that information is already in the public sphere. She will not do anything that could potentially give the U.S. government opportunity to undermine her or her achievements to date. Her one action outside formal procedure is the metal kangaroo badge permanently pinned to her lapel, a silent protest of the "kangaroo court" style of justice her clients are being subjected to.

As a young woman growing up in Texas in the 1950s, she was no stranger to injustice. At age ten, she was the only student in a class debate who supported the *Brown v. Board of Education* court case, which said that segregated public schools were unconstitutional. Her teachers called her parents to say they were worried about her for being so strident. But as *"intellectual lefties,"* they supported her. At seventeen, she would follow police paddy wagons around Chicago at night, taking photos of cops beating up people. She has been arrested on three separate occasions for peaceful protest, and has spent her entire life fighting for the rights of people, irrespective of what those people may or may not have done. She's a small woman, but she stands tall and resolute in front of power.

What comes out in our conversation is that Nancy is an avid practitioner of martial arts, jiu-jitsu in particular, and she uses the principles taught by her sensei in taking on opponents much bigger than herself:

> *"Whatever you do, do it with intent. In martial arts, we call it 'one plus one.' Just one good kick and one good punch is better than twenty you didn't have any intent behind. Do not say something unless you mean it, do not do something unless you are committed. Do not confront by shouting, but confront by using your intellectual powers and the power of a better argument, by standing your ground, by keeping your center, by never transgressing*

so they cannot attack. Ultimately, the trick is to absorb and redirect their energy. You use their own power against themselves."

None of this is at small cost to herself. Her tireless work has meant she's been accused of being a terrorist sympathizer or a flat-out terrorist, purely for her insistence that the government follow its own Constitution and prosecute people fairly. She says that the people who have criticized her the most savagely have been those within, or connected to, the Bush administration— which she says is ironic, as they are the ones who, by falsifying reports, condoning torture, and signing off on extraordinary renditions, broke the law. And who, therefore, one day may need her services most. Absorb and redirect indeed.

"Whatever you do, do it with intent. . . . Just one good kick and one good punch is better than twenty you didn't have any intent behind. Do not say something unless you mean it, do not do something unless you are committed."

—*Nancy Hollander*

JUDE'S LAW

ON THE DAY WE MEET, time is running out for Jude Law. Not in respect to life generally, but on his parking meter. To avoid the hassle of finding loose change and reparking, we decide to sit and talk in his car, pulled up on the side of Shaftesbury Avenue, a kind of poor man's *Carpool Karaoke*.

We chat about our respective childhoods. I mention I grew up in Huddersfield, and to my surprise, Jude says he's going there that weekend. No disrespect to my hometown, but it's not normally a place where international movie stars go to hang out. When I ask what will take him there, he explains it's to meet with the uncle of a young Syrian boy Jude befriended when he visited The Jungle, the makeshift refugee camp in Calais. The child refugee in question had seen his mom, dad, and siblings die in the crossing from Africa and was in the camp all alone, so Jude offered to pay the legal fees and oversee the process of getting him out of the camp and into the arms of his one remaining family member up in Huddersfield.

The fact that Jude went several times to the refugee camp in the first place, is doing all this personally for the young lad, and, most tellingly, it only comes up in conversation because of an unlikely coincidence says a lot about the guy offscreen.

In fact, Jude Law has a long history of going the extra mile to support important causes. On previous occasions he traveled to the Democratic Republic of the Congo and to Afghanistan with the peacemaking organization Peace One Day; he was part of an initiative that managed to broker a twenty-four-hour cease-fire agreement between the Taliban and the American military in Afghanistan, the result being that during the brief cessation 10,000 health workers were mobilized. They inoculated 1.4 million children.

He puts his track record of stepping out of the limelight and into pretty tough places down to several things. One is to make sense of this strange thing called fame. *"I'm in no way comparing myself to him, but my hero John Lennon said, 'If you're going to poke a camera in my face, then I am going to say something important.' That's the worth of media and fame, to help important things get noticed."* He also says if he were to stick to just the movie-star life of five-star hotels and VIP experiences, then he would *"feel fat with guilt."* On the most basic level, he has a curiosity about the world and a desire to engage with as many different aspects of it as possible. His perspective is essentially *"Why wouldn't you want to go to these places?"*

This ethos of experiencing life for its own sake is echoed in his advice for people who want to make it as an actor. *"There is such a large amount of luck needed to get your moment, so you have to be in acting for the right reasons: do it because you love the thing, the process, because you'll enjoy doing a no-pay play in a room above a pub. You have to be happy doing it that way, because what happens otherwise if you don't get your break?"* He says it is having that love of the actual thing that will keep you sane if you do make it because otherwise *"it can fast start to feel like a business and you will need to keep that original flame alight or you can lose your way."*

When I ask for his single best piece of wisdom, we revert back to talking about his childhood, and he credits his dad with his favorite advice, given to him as a young boy:

"If you are going to be late, enjoy being late."

It was advice he meant literally: that if you are late, rather than panic and stress, enjoy the extra time it's affording you. But it has also served Jude as a wider metaphor for life, reminding him to *"relish the moment, be in the moment, do the right thing in the moment, whatever that moment is,"* whether in a refugee camp, in a room above a pub, or on the set of your latest blockbuster.

And with that, he has to go. He's running late.

"If you are late, enjoy

going to be being late."

—*Jude Law*

AHMED "KATHY" KATHRADA AND DENIS GOLDBERG, FREEDOM FIGHTERS

I enter a Mayfair hotel room to interview Ahmed "Kathy" Kathrada and Denis Goldberg, two of Nelson Mandela's fellow Freedom Fighters, who stood trial and were imprisoned with him for nearly three decades of hard labor. The first thing that is pointed out to me is the modestly sized bed.

"That bed is bigger than the cells we were kept in on Robben Island for twenty-seven years."

In a small, simple way, it brings to mind some of the deprivations these men endured in dedicating their lives to fighting apartheid in South Africa.

Between them they have experienced the worst of what humans do to one another—torture, violence, the murdering of loved ones, unjust imprisonment, solitary confinement, thirty years of separation from their families (Denis's wife was allowed to visit twice in the whole period of his imprisonment).

Despite these experiences, not once did they withdraw from the fight. They made a pledge as young men to overthrow apartheid, and they spent every waking hour of the next sixty years doing just that.

So where did this commitment and resilience come from?

Kathy can pinpoint the moment. He was twenty-two, on a visit to Auschwitz as a young man after the end of the Second World War. Here, among the profoundly disturbing reality of what had happened (evidenced by the human bones still scattered casually around the ground), a dark truth dawned upon him. *"Stood there, I realized that the logical conclusion of racism was genocide. It became clear to me we had to end apartheid to prevent the same happening to the South African people."* After what he saw, and comprehending it, he knew he had to take on the fight and never give it up.

An understanding of the history of man's struggle for freedom also helped to form their resolve. Denis recounts that as a young white man, he was raised by socially aware parents who not only made sure he respected all people who came to their house, irrespective of color, but also educated him about the Gandhi-led movement for Indian independence, told tales of the lesser-known German resistance, and explained the hundred years of struggle by indigenous South Africans against British colonization. These stories of resistance against an oppressor inspired him and showed him that freedom was not only worth fighting for, it could also ultimately be won.

They are two of the most remarkable men imaginable. As they recount without any bitterness the extreme costs of their sixty-year fight, the humor remains constant—*"How did you manage to cope with the hardship of prison?" "We got lots of practice."*—and their energy and fight are undimmed.

The morning before we met, Denis had been invited to

10 Downing Street to meet David Cameron. Denis's opening salvo to the prime minister: *"So when are you bloody Imperial Brits going to stop beating up on South Africa?"*

Denis is the more fiery of the two gentlemen. In some ways his story is even more pronounced, as he was a white man fighting for an end to apartheid, which was virtually unheard of and meant he was shunned by his own community in a way the other fighters were not. But all men paid the same price for fighting for freedom: life imprisonment.

Even worse had been expected. During the infamous Rivonia court case (1963–64), where Denis, Kathy, Nelson Mandela, Andrew Mlangeni, and others stood trial for their action against the South African apartheid regime, everyone thought they would receive the death penalty. They knew when they'd signed up for their campaign that it was the most likely outcome.

Following a three-hour speech by Nelson Mandela, the final verdict shocked everyone: life imprisonment. When Denis's mother, who was hard of hearing, called from the gallery, *"What is it? What's the verdict?"* Denis replied, *"It's life. Life is wonderful!"*—a response that gives a sense of the undying resilience and granite-hewn optimism of the men.

An uncomfortable lump in my throat forms as I consider that this moment of relief was then followed by more than twenty years in prison, and they experienced the hardest of incarcerations. Understandably, they prefer to dwell on the outcome, not the experience. The victory, not the battle.

So I ask them about how they'd achieved their success. What brought about the end of apartheid? With total clarity, the men cite four factors: the armed struggle, which meant the government undermined itself by spending more and more money on fighting its own people; their role as political prisoners, which gave the movement the angle that respected figureheads were being unjustly treated; the international solidarity movement, in which governments and civil organizations boycotted South Africa and signaled their opposition to the regime; and finally, the people's struggle in South Africa—the United Democratic Front, trade unions, and civic organizations—the majority of the country coming together to protest, to disrupt, to say *"No more."*

Kathy is clear that, of the four aspects, the people's struggle was the most important. As Nelson Mandela said to the minister of justice from his prison cell in Robben Island, *"The future of South Africa can be by bloodshed, and in the end the majority will win, or it can be by a negotiated settlement."* With the majority of the people actively protesting and pushing for change, the government eventually conceded.

When I ask what has been the main lesson from their most remarkable of lives, the answers are the most profound of all I have heard.

From Denis:

> **"I am going to quote John Stuart Mills from the mouth of Nelson Mandela: 'To be free, it is not sufficient to cast off your chains; you must so live that you respect and enhance the freedom of others.' It's the same concept of**

what Archbishop Desmond Tutu calls Ubuntu. I am who I am only through others in society. We're humans in the end, and that's what it's all about."

And then Kathy quietly, gently, definitively states his truth:

"And ultimately, the fight for justice will inevitably lead to success. No matter what the sacrifices are."

As these men have known.

LILY EBERT,
AUSCHWITZ SURVIVOR

"*WE WEREN'T SEEN AS ENEMIES; we weren't seen as humans—to the Nazis, we were just cockroaches. They completely industrialized their killing of us.*"

I'm talking with Lily Ebert in a quiet room in North London's Holocaust Survivors Centre, the first of its kind in the world. Lily is a proud, defiant, eloquent lady, but as she recounts her experience of Auschwitz, she pauses many times. Seventy years on, the pain of mankind's most horrific genocide remains acute. As Lily says, *"It is very difficult to explain something that is unexplainable."*

"The lucky ones died" is her reflection on the transportation to Auschwitz: hundreds of people rammed into railway cattle trucks in the heat of summer, with no food or water for five days, surrounded by the dead bodies of those who didn't make it. Lily recounts the last thing her mother did before the train arrived. She made Lily swap shoes with her. Hidden within the heel was a small piece of gold, the last of their family's possessions. Call it a mother's intuition: when they arrived at Auschwitz, Dr. Mengele, the Angel of Death, separated the masses into two groups—half

were sent to the left, to what would be their immediate death in the gas chambers, and the others were sent to the right, to the slow death of starvation in the camp. Lily's last memory of her mother and younger brother and sister is of them being pushed to the left.

Inside the camp, Lily and her two other younger sisters were stripped of their clothes and dressed in rags, fed on one piece of bread a day, and housed in sheds crammed with ten times the number of people they were built for. Every day there were constant "selections," in which anyone deemed not fit enough to work was sent off to the crematorium next door.

Lily says the worst thing of all was the terrible smell emitted from that factory-like building, with the chimney that smoked twenty-four hours a day. It was only when she asked some fellow campmates what was made there that people explained it wasn't a factory; it was where they burned Jews, and the only way out of Auschwitz was up that chimney. *We told them they were mad, that we didn't believe them. But very quickly we found out it was true.*

In the hell of this experience, Lily promised herself that if she did somehow manage to survive, she would spend the rest of her life telling people about Auschwitz so it couldn't happen again. It's a promise she is keeping for the thousandth time by telling me her story today. That sense of purpose and the responsibility she felt to look after her two younger sisters gave her reason to stay alive in a place where she would otherwise rather have been dead.

It also gives context to one of the pieces of advice she wants to pass on: *"To always have hope against hope. I was as down as a human being can go, but look at me, I survived. I have gone from nearly starving to death to, seventy years later, being sent to meet the Queen and being given a British Empire Medal. So no matter how bad the situation, try to do what you can and don't give up."* However, her most precious piece of advice:

"Make always the best from what you have, no matter how little it is."

She brings the thought alive by referring back to that one piece of bread a day they each had to survive on. *"Some in the camp could not make the best of it—they ate it in a second, and they dreamed to have something else, but there was nothing else, and they were the ones that didn't survive. I would always eat the one piece of bread as slowly as possible and keep some for the morning hidden under my arm. And that helped me survive."*

At the end of our meeting, Lily proudly shows me a small gold pendant hanging from a chain around her neck, which she has worn every day since she was freed. She explains it is the piece of gold that her mother had hidden in her shoe, which Lily had managed to keep hidden throughout her whole time in Auschwitz.

I reflect on what this piece of gold and its owner have seen and had to endure. The starvation, the brutal conditions, the worst of mankind. But it also creates a small question in my mind: given that she lost her shoes in the camp, how did she manage to keep the piece of gold? Eyes sparkling with triumph, Lily says: *"I told you—you have to make the best of whatever you have. The only thing I had was that piece of bread, so I hid the gold every night in that and they never spotted it. I was cleverer than them."*

Lily Ebert: pure gold.

"Make always the best from what you have, no matter how little it is. . . . I would always eat the one piece of bread as slowly as possible and keep some for the morning hidden under my arm. And that helped me survive."

—*Lily Ebert*

THE HEARTBREAKING GENIUS OF RICHARD CURTIS

I F THE OSCARS HAD A category for Best Human, Richard Curtis would get nominated. Not for the pleasure his script-writing has brought to the masses—abundant though that is, with *Four Weddings and a Funeral*; *Notting Hill; Love, Actually*; and other such treasures to his name—but for his decades-long commitment as cofounder, leader, and/or chief agitator for such era-defining social initiatives as Comic Relief, Red Nose Day, Make Poverty History, and Live 8. No other person has done more to make development aid and charity part of the mainstream.

From such an evolved human being, I have high hopes for his best piece of advice, especially when he says he's thought about it in advance and committed his wisdom to paper. *"So here it is,"* he says as he opens his writerly, leather-bound notebook. He sits forward, clears his throat, and announces:

"Don't let your mum cut your hair. That's important."

Closes book, sits back.

He's serious, sort of. *"My mum did mine once and I didn't talk to her for three weeks."* This recollection triggers a follow-up insight. *"And if you're a mum, don't cut your son's hair, he'll hate you."*

It's not just his wisdom on hairdos that is rooted in childhood; most key attributes of his life have an invisible string that, when pulled, brings up a story from his younger years. He confesses to having scripted so many romantic movies *"because I had my heart broken at university,"* and he writes a "hapless Bernard" into every movie, an in-joke revenge on a man who had once stolen his girlfriend.

More significantly, it was during one of his younger, lovestruck, feeling-sorry-for-himself moments that his father said something that changed Richard's perspective on life in general. *"My dad, not unkindly, described his own life at eighteen, which was finding himself fatherless and cleaning toilets on a ship to earn money, and compared it to what my life was like. And I was absolutely fixed after that. It gave me a sense of perspective between my problems and other people's that I have kept forever."*

A second slice of childhood wisdom from his dad has also reverberated through his life: *"He always said you can't be happier than happy."* The idea is that if you are content and things are good, do not be disturbed by the possibility that they could be better. *"Don't let a lovely day out in the countryside be ruined by the fact that it's not sunny."*

As with his movies, though, there is a twist. *"I say that, but I am an unhappy person almost all the time."* I assume he's joking, but in response to my protestations he explains that raising money for the development of the world's poorest nations means he gets his heart rebroken several times a day.

"With the charity work, I feel the pressure of every phone call, that if I can talk this person into doing something, kids survive; if I don't,

they won't. Just today I got a call from a lovely guy saying he won't be able to do a sketch [for the show] and of course I have to lie and say, 'It's OK, you helped last year,' but inside I am dying."

So his best piece of advice comes directly from his experience of trying to change the world, but also reflects the frustration and heartbreak that comes from knowing that people talk a good game but often fail to help when the need for aid is so vast.

> **"None of us should ever underestimate our ability to change people's lives. There is a direct cause and effect of what we do here and what happens there. But if you want to help, you have to actually do something. You can't just talk about it. My motto is 'If you want to make things happen, you have to make things.' Create an object, a slogan, a film, a little book, a badge, a hashtag, a Red Nose Day . . . make something so wonderful that it captures people's hearts and minds so they can't help but be dragged in and help. And even better, make it funny too. That's all I have ever done."**

And there is no one who does it better.

NOËLLA COURSARIS MUSUNKA, MODEL CITIZEN

THE DEMOCRATIC REPUBLIC OF THE Congo is a contradiction rendered as a country. It has more natural resources than any other nation in the world, but is one of the poorest in gross domestic product and life expectancy. It has enough latent hydropower to fuel most of Africa, but less than 10 percent of homes have electricity. It has an image in the West of a barren, war-stricken land of heinous crimes, but is one of the most verdant and beautiful countries you could ever hope to visit, with people as friendly and welcoming as any on Earth, a fact I can attest to, not just from having spent time there, but also because I have sat opposite one of the DRC's favorite daughters.

The lady in question is Noëlla Coursaris Musunka, the international model who splits her time between fashion shoots for *Vogue* and Agent Provocateur and her parallel life running Malaika, an organization she founded, which provides education and schooling to young girls in the DRC.

Noëlla's backstory is that of a woman who has known tough times. She was born to a desperately poor family in the Congo and lost her father at the age of five. In a country where 7 million kids don't go to school and where life expectancy is just forty-eight years, her mother took the understandable decision to send Noëlla to be raised by her aunt in Europe. But Noëlla never forgot her childhood and her home, and she has used the currency of her modeling career to become one of the brightest lights and biggest advocates for her country of birth.

She was motivated to combine her career in fashion with tackling education in the DRC for defiantly positive reasons. *"I'm a spokesperson for the beliefs that I want for my country. I want children to be taught that they are living in an amazing country, on an amazing continent—that we have nothing to envy in any way."* At the sharper end, she also wants the people of the Congo to benefit more from the resources of their country. *"If you get on a plane in the Congo, it's full of Americans, English, Chinese, and Indians, but very few Africans. It's mad. It seems a lot of people love our resources!"* she says, laughing, but she means it.

Ultimately, Noëlla wants to help end the era in which Africa is treated as "less than" by the rest of the world, and to do that, education is the answer. *"Through quality education, our own people can become agents of change, become leaders of their own country, so we can work with the West as equals. That is what's missing."*

She makes no boast about the scale of her work. At the end of the day, she is educating only thousands of children in a country that is failing millions, but it's a start. And she uses her voice and the platform of her career to agitate others to do the same. This mission of encouraging others to act, to get involved, to do something rather than nothing, is inherent in her advice.

"Any voice you have in this world, you have to use it. Whatever money you have the day you die, you die without it, so donate it. If you can only give an hour of your time, then do that."

—*Noëlla Coursaris Musunka*

UP ALL NIGHT
WITH INDRA NOOYI

WHAT DO YOU DO WHEN "the Most Powerful Woman in the World," as ranked by *Forbes*, invites you to dinner? You say yes, of course. The woman in question was Indra Nooyi, the Global CEO of PepsiCo and board member of the Federal Reserve. The context was that Innocent, the juice business started by myself and two friends, had been growing fast and, unknown to us, had gotten us on the radar of some of the major food and drink companies. Indra's people called us out of the blue and said she would like to meet. They suggested dinner next time she was in London.

It seemed churlish to say no, and I was curious about what it took to be a global CEO of a business responsible for operations across the planet, with hundreds of thousands of employees, creating opportunities and issues in every time zone. How did she manage the workload? What was life like? Did she have any good advice? The dinner proved illuminating on all three fronts.

We started the evening with polite chitchat, with questions like *"So how long are you in London for?"* and other such conversational standbys. Interestingly, it turned out Indra was leaving that evening, as soon as we finished dinner. Her private jet was fired up and ready to go and would be heading from London to New York after our coffee and mints. Meanwhile, her husband, another global CEO of a big tech company, had his private jet in New York also ready to go, destination: London. They had two daughters and a rule—that one parent should always be at home with them, and they timed their flights so that when she took off, he would too. At around 1 A.M. that night, somewhere above the Atlantic, they would pass each other at a combined velocity of 1,000 miles per hour, like proverbial (and extremely fast) ships in the night. I found the image memorable. As I did the idea of a two-jet household.

When we got on to Indra's approach to work, she spoke with total passion. She deeply loved what she did, and she did it a lot. At one point in the conversation, she asked, *"You know that buzz you get when you haven't been to sleep for three nights because you've been working on a deal?"* I had to admit to her I did not. In fact, I said, I didn't even know what the buzz from staying up for just one night was like—well, not for work, anyway—an answer that momentarily perplexed her.

She told me that she'd once done eight nights straight without going to bed, such was the size of the deal she was working on. I queried whether this was even physiologically possible, and she admitted, under my cross-examination, she had grabbed fifteen minutes on her office couch on the eighth night. To this day, I still don't know if she was playing mind games with me. If she was, it worked. I thought if that's what it takes to be a global CEO, I'd better stay a local one.

She was brilliant company: charming, eloquent, engaging—and capable of saying the most unexpected things. When I got to asking for her advice, she first wanted to dispense a few leadership tips, the most memorable of which was *"I get my board to come round to my house once a month and I print out song sheets and we all sing songs together. I really recommend you do the same."* When I said I wanted her most valuable piece of advice, this is what she offered:

> **"Don't take holidays. When you get to my age, you will regret taking them. Give yourself a maximum of a day or a day and a half a year. And use that to read books on your industry. The rest of the time you should just work."**

The first thing I thought was *"Wow, that's genuinely the worst piece of advice I've ever heard."* The second thing I thought was *"You need to go on holiday more often."* I was going to say just that, but then with my third thought, I remembered that she was "the Most Powerful Woman in the World," so I just kept quiet, nodded, and ate my pudding.

"Don't take holidays. When you get to my age, you will regret taking them. Give yourself a maximum of a day or a day and a half a year. And use that to read books on your industry. The rest of the time you should just work."

—*Indra Nooyi*

FACE TIME WITH UELI STECK

THE NORTH FACE OF THE Eiger is the most infamous climb in the world. It's known in the mountaineering community as The Wall of Death: a mile-high, concave cliff face covered with ice, loose rocks, and tragedy. It's as difficult and unforgiving to climb as it sounds and looks.

The first two people ever to attempt climbing it died trying. And so did the next four, starting a death tally that, at upwards of sixty people, has continued to rise. When a group did eventually reach the summit of the north face, it had taken them more than three days. I give this historical context because Ueli Steck, the Swiss climber I'm currently with, recently did it in under three hours, an unimaginable speed made possible only by his gravity- (and sanity-) defying decision to do it without ropes. It was an achievement so disproportionate, so unprecedented in the annals of mountaineering, that it didn't just rewrite the rules of climbing; it seemed to also rewrite the laws of physics.

As an amateur climber myself (and I strongly emphasize the word "amateur"), I tell him I struggle with his decision to climb without ropes, which are the only hope you have of remaining safe if you make a mistake and fall (which, in my experience, happens often).

"I remember when I started climbing and I heard there were people climbing without ropes, I thought to myself, that's insane, I will never do that. But it's a process, figuring out stuff, doing it better, and that's what drives me."

But what about the chance element you can't control? *"You just have to accept it, you have to commit."* And the fear? *"When I'm climbing, there is no fear. If you feel fear, it's because you're not well prepared."*

As advice goes, it sounds potentially like bravado, but in Ueli's case, it's not. In fact, in Ueli's view, having bravado is deadly: you need an absence of ego to stay safe. *"You have to make sure you feel no pressure to get to the top—otherwise, you start making the wrong decisions. On a climbing day, I always say, 'I'll just go and have a look.' I never say, 'I am going to do it.' And if I have a bad feeling, I just come back down. I believe if you stick to that, then you never make a mistake."*

Of course, with Ueli's approach to climbing, there literally can never be a mistake, not one.

"I really play on the edge. The time on the Eiger, I had to move fast, so I allow myself to hit only once with the ice axe—no compromise, never twice. Full commitment each time I place the axe. And it works. You really concentrate, you really hit precise."

It's a way of thinking that turns inside out what other human beings would do. If you were a mile up a vertical cliff face and your life depended on the ice axe you're about to put all your weight on, you'd want to check that it would hold. Ueli instead uses the consequences of what it would mean if it won't, to make sure he concentrates hard enough to place it correctly in the first place. That is some advanced psychology.

On a deeper level, that degree of commitment is perhaps partly enabled by his personal take on the potential consequence. *"If I fuck up, it's over. I'm dead and I don't have to live with my mistake."* Amazingly, he says he would rather have that outcome than, say, the pressure of being a CEO, *"where if you screw up, you have to fire people and they lose their jobs and you know it was your fault and you have to live with that your whole lifetime. I don't know if I could handle that."*

It's a final comment that reinforces the huge gap between myself and Ueli. I have actually climbed the Eiger—it took me two days, and was on the incomparably easier western ridge, and involved a lot of ropes and guides, and there were still plenty of moments when, clinging trembling to the rock, I would have happily fired my own grandmother to get off that damn mountain. But I decide not to mention that.

Not long after our conversation, on April 30, 2017, Ueli Steck fell to his death while climbing alone in the Himalayas as part of acclimization preparation for a second summiting of Everest. The loss to the mountaineering community is immense, his contribution to it even greater.

THE TWO VOICES OF
ANNIE LENNOX

ANNIE LENNOX HAS TWO VOICES. The first is the one that has sold over 80 million albums, winning her five Grammys, an Academy Award, and more Brit Awards than any other female artist. Her second voice is the one she lends to women's rights and the issue of HIV/AIDS in Africa. And it's this campaigning voice that takes center stage these days.

Annie remembers the moment when her singing voice changed pitch from artistry to activism. It was after taking part in a concert to launch 46664, Nelson Mandela's HIV/AIDS foundation in South Africa, the country with the highest rate of HIV infection in the world. She witnessed Mandela describe the HIV pandemic as *"a silent genocide, carrying the face of women."* He explained that one in three pregnant women were HIV-positive in South Africa, and AIDS was (and still is) a leading cause of death for women of reproductive age globally. Then, on a visit to a township hospital, she saw the impact of AIDS for herself—in clinics, rape-crisis centers, orphanages, and people's homes. It was a dark epiphany for Annie. From then on, she shaped her life around responding to the tragedy.

The result has been over a decade of tireless work on tackling the issue—a work that has, according to Archbishop Desmond Tutu, *"contributed significantly to turning the pandemic around in our country."* In 2007 she founded a campaign called SING to raise global awareness and prompt action, helping to ensure that HIV-positive women and children have access to the treatment and care they need. Annie has traveled across the globe giving fundraising performances, presentations, speeches, and interviews on radio and television, and in the printed press, at conferences and rallies, and in government buildings, speaking truth to power at every given opportunity. She also became the founder of The Circle, an organization that aims to inspire and connect women in order to harness their skills, creativity, and influence, and to transform the challenges and injustices faced by the most disempowered girls and women in the world.

Those dusty plains of sub-Saharan Africa are a long way from the working-class tenement block in Aberdeen where she was raised. Coming from a poor but musical family, she studied the piano and flute at school, which led her to be offered a place at the Royal Academy of Music in London at the age of seventeen. *"It became my passport out of there."*

Tough years followed, however. *"I had very little money and didn't really know anyone. I lived in a variety of different bedsits, doing whatever I could to make ends meet, but even though my chances seemed bleak, I didn't want to go back to Scotland and feel as if I'd failed."*

One constant through it all was singing. *"I would sing and sing and sing, walking down the street, in the shower, all the time, just by myself, and by the time three years at the Royal Academy had come to an end, I knew I wanted to be a singer-songwriter, so I started to write songs on an old Victorian harmonium. I'd been writing poems since I was twelve, and I had a lot to say."*

But for all the hard work, practice, and passion, one factor for success was still missing: serendipity. That came thanks to Camden Market, where Annie sold secondhand clothes, sharing a stall with a friend. It was there that she got to know a guy selling records who told her, *"You should meet my mate, Dave."* According to Annie, there was a creative connection with Dave Stewart from the beginning, and within a few years they were dominating the charts on both sides of the Atlantic as the Eurythmics.

Her life story is of a woman following her passions, wherever they may take her, from the tenements of Aberdeen to the townships of Africa, via the Grammys in America, and her advice fits that story perfectly.

> *"There will be 'Aha!' moments in life when a light might go on, when you think to yourself, 'I MUST do that'—whatever it is. It's not because someone says you should do it, but it's because you feel absolutely compelled to and there would be something wrong with the world if you didn't. If you find that light—acknowledge it. Find other people who share that passion. Cultivate it. Find that deeper purpose in your life."*

As voices go, it's a good one to listen to.

INSIDE HESTON BLUMENTHAL

I T'S NOT GOING WELL. THE score is 10 to 1, match point to Heston Blumenthal. The Michelin three-starred chef and owner of the best restaurant in the world (as voted for by the best chefs in the world) turns out to also be a fiend at table tennis. In my defense, before the match started, he plied me with strange-colored cocktails and confessed to having table-tennis lessons up to three times a week. At least the humiliation is swift: his final serve goes the way we both know it's going to, and I retire to the bench and to the solace of my next cocktail.

The experience of going to see Heston at home is the British middle-class equivalent of visiting Hunter S. Thompson: liquor is drunk, cigars are smoked, deep chats are had, and while no guns get fired, he does have his table-tennis serving machine, a device that shoots out 100 balls a minute. We turn it on and it causes a hailstorm of the little blighters pinging off every wall and surface in his basement, which is dedicated to table tennis.

I've known Heston for a while now. His brain is like that ping-pong machine, capable of throwing out 100 ideas a minute. His curiosity, creativity, and appetite for learning are greater than in anyone I know. The first time we met was at a company meeting, where I watched him get 300 people to each eat an apple holding their noses, to demonstrate how flavor is what we smell, not what we taste. He is a man who lives and literally breathes sensory experiences. And to illustrate the point, we're now back in his kitchen and he's teaching me how to smoke a cigar so you can appreciate all the different flavors. It involves repeatedly pulling a lit cigar from his lips with a pronounced "schmack" sound; the trick apparently is to *"keep the smoke out of your mouth, don't let it get past your teeth."*

Food doesn't just play a central role in Heston's life—he sees it as a way of explaining all of human existence; food has shaped not just what we do and who we are, but also *what* we are.

"We evolved because of eating and the things around eating . . . when we discovered fire, we moved away from eating only raw starches, our lower digestion started to shrink, our neck and therefore our larynx lengthened, which allowed us over time to start to vocalize. And that ability to communicate meant we could start to spread ideas, build up our imaginations, and from that everything became possible."

Connecting food to human imagination is his signature dish. He's brought more original ideas into the kitchen than anyone else. He first got major attention in the culinary world when his restaurant, The Fat Duck, put crab ice cream on the menu—a dish that now seems almost ordinary in the food fantasy world he's since created of edible pubs: food you can listen to and chocolates that float in midair.

He says his interest in the world of food went from zero to one hundred in a lunchtime: when Heston was a teenager, his dad got a bonus from work and to celebrate he took the family to a Michelin three-starred restaurant in France. The combination of not just the food and the tastes, but the sensory overload of the smell of lavender from the restaurant garden, the feel of linen on the table, the crunch of gravel underfoot, the sounds of crickets and clinking glasses: *"It felt like I'd gone down this rabbit hole into Wonderland and I found something that fascinated me and I knew right then I wanted to be a chef."*

His imagination and curiosity were kick-started by studying ice cream. He found a recipe from 1870 for Parmesan ice cream. *"I thought, 'That's bizarre!' and then I started questioning why was it bizarre; who says ice cream has to be sweet? And once I started questioning that, I began questioning everything. I found that thread and just kept on pulling."*

It means that while your average chef is checking out other restaurants and menus for inspiration, Heston will be investigating the worlds of biology, chemistry, history, and geography. He has teamed up with professors in macrobiotics, as well as psychologists and molecular scientists. As an example of how deep he can go into these lines of inquiry, the Royal Society of Chemists published a list of 175 of the most influential scientists and chemists on the planet, alive or dead. Einstein is on it, and so is Heston. He leads me over to a coat of arms he created, now framed on the kitchen wall. He says it took him seven years to design, as he wanted to capture everything he stood for. There is a twig of lavender to reflect smell and the trip to that first restaurant, a pair of hands to reflect the craft of his work, a Tudor rose for the historical element of his cooking, a magnifying glass for the importance of investigation and inquiry, and an apple to reflect Newton's discovery and nonlinear thinking. Most telling of all is his motto, just two words and inscribed in italic font, which explains his approach and creativity and what he puts forward as his best piece of advice for life:

"Question everything."

And to me he expands:

"The opposite of question everything is question nothing. And if you don't question things, there's no knowledge, no learning, no creativity, no freedom of choice, no imagination. So I always ask why. And why not. I ask question, question, question, question. And then I listen. And that's how I discover something new."

He then concludes by asking *me* a question. It's the one I am most dreading: *"Fancy another game of table tennis?"*

"Question everything. . . .
If you don't question things,
there's no knowledge,
no learning, no creativity,
no freedom of choice,
no imagination."

—*Heston Blumenthal*

GLOVES OFF WITH LAILA ALI

W HEN I SPEAK TO LAILA Ali, the most successful
female boxer in history, she's having her nails done.
She is in the make-up chair getting suitably
glammed up to record an episode of her popular lifestyle TV
show. It's a big change from her fighting career: boxing gloves
have been replaced by manicures, ring time for screen time, and
black eyes for black eyeliner. Although it has to be said, as an
undisputed four-time world champion and the winner of all
twenty-four of her twenty-four professional fights (twenty-one
by knockout), black eyes and bruises were mainly the other
fighters' problem.

"The first thing you should know about me is I am a very ambitious
person, willing to do the hours and whatever it takes," Laila states in
a straight, no-nonsense reply when I ask what it takes to become
a world champion. No one gets to the top without the hard
work, I say, but I'm curious where the drive and necessary
ambition come from. Her response is candid, open, brave. *"As*
a kid I learned the only person I could always depend on was me. There
were too many times waiting outside school to be picked up and no one
would show up, so I learned to say, "Fuck this, this isn't happening"

and I would walk home alone. I learned that I had to make things happen for myself." Interestingly, that ambition wasn't first channeled into boxing. *"My thing was nails. At age 16 I decided I wanted to open a nail business. Be the CEO. Grow it big. So I went to beauty school to learn how to do it."* And that was what she was doing, until she discovered boxing.

People probably assume Laila decided to become a fighter because of her father, but until she was eighteen being a boxer never crossed her mind. The idea only came to her when she was flicking through the TV channels one night and saw women sparring. *"Until then, I had never given boxing a thought. But when I saw those women with gloves on fighting, it made me sit up."*

Yet it still took Laila a year before she would even walk into a gym and pick up a pair of gloves—a year of debating with herself over whether or not she should. *"It wasn't the path I was on. I didn't want to be in the public eye, so I practically talked myself out of it."*

I'm curious why she didn't just give it a try to see if she liked it. But it turns out that is not how Laila Ali approaches things. *"Oh no. If I am going to do something, then I am all in. I knew if I was going to box, I would have to become a world champion. And I knew how much work that would entail. So I had to be sure before I even started."*

So after that year of contemplation, she decided she would do it. She didn't tell her dad. Deliberately keeping things low profile, Laila did her research, found a gym and the right trainer, and started getting on with it. And while there were no shortcuts, just hours and hours of work, sweat, and pain, Laila Ali was a natural. *"It felt right for me to fight. It awoke this intensity and anger in me. I have a mean streak in me, which you gotta have for certain moments in the ring."* As each one of her twenty-two opponents found out.

There came, of course, the time she did have to tell her dad. If she'd been hoping that he'd be happy that she was carrying on the family legacy, she was disappointed. *"He said I shouldn't do it, that boxing isn't for women. It's too tough. That I was going to get hurt. But rather than get offended or angry, I just thought 'I'll show you.'"* And, boy, did she!

Life is different now. She's hung up her gloves. And she's gone back to her first dream, to be the successful CEO of her own beauty business—as well as a bestselling author, TV host, actor, mom . . . the list continues.

Does she miss the fighting?

> **"Boxing was good for me. It was a great outlet. But you have got to be willing to change. I can't be the same person as I was when I was twenty-five and fighting."** But the same will to win burns on. **"With my new career, I still have my goals and my plans. I'm still prepared to do whatever needs to be done and to the best I possibly can."**

Laila's best piece of advice taps into this commitment to strive, to excel, to win.

> **"We all have what it takes, inside us. Trust yourself, trust your intuition. Don't let someone else be in control**

of your destiny, and don't not go after your passion because of fear. Look fear in the eyes and say, 'I am coming for you.'"

Since we are talking about fear, I ask what was inside her head before she stepped into the ring each time to fight. What does an undisputed world champion tell herself? *"I would always be confident because I was so well prepared. I did the training, studied the form, would be in great condition. I always knew I was going to win. It was just a question of finding out in which round."*

Laila Ali pauses, and then says, *"And as the last little cherry on top, just before I stepped into that ring, I would also say, 'Oh, and I also happen to be the daughter of the greatest fighter of all time.' And then the bell would go, and I would fight."*

Ding, ding.

"We all have what it takes, inside us. Trust yourself, trust your intuition. Don't let someone else be in control of your destiny, and don't not go after your passion because of fear. Look fear in the eyes and say, 'I am coming for you.'"

—*Laila Ali*

JONY IVE JUST SAYS NO

O
UTSIDE SPORTS, IT'S HARD TO claim that someone is
genuinely number one in their respective field. How
can you judge who is the best artist, writer, actor, or
whatever in the world? Jony Ive, the head of design at Apple Inc.
and the most successful industrial designer of the modern age, is
an exception to this dilemma. He is the man who crafted that
convergence of artistry and technology currently residing in your
pocket, and who worked with the world's most famous and
revered founder to create literally the most valuable company
in existence.

For a man who genuinely is the Big I Am, he doesn't act like
it. I meet him at a burger truck eating some fries. Admittedly,
it's a burger truck at a private party, and they are very nice fries,
but with his extraordinary success also comes a high degree of
humility and self-deprecation. It seems to be a trait among
genuinely successful and credible people: they tend to be, for
want of a better description, nice. He even offered me some of
his fries.

I decline on the food; I ask for his number-one piece of advice
instead. It's neither original nor complicated, but is probably the

most important driver of success—and certainly fits with the laserlike focus of his company:

> *"You have to really focus. Just do one thing. And aim to become best in the world at it."*

He admits that wasn't necessarily how he used to think. With a brain as creative as Jony's, there are a thousand different things he would want to do. *"I learned the importance of focus from Steve [Jobs]. His view was you have to say no a lot more often than you say yes. In fact, he used to ask me each day what I had said no to, to check that I was stopping things and saying no to things and not getting distracted."*

My favorite part of this story is that when Jony told it to me, he paused and then confessed that he used to make up projects that he could tell Steve he'd stopped, so he always had an example of something he'd said no to when Steve came by. That brings me to a second thing about successful people, even the brilliant ones: like the rest of us, they are, at times, still faking it a little.

"Just do one thing.
And aim to become best
in the world at it."

—*Jony Ive*

LORD WAHEED ALLI,
CHAMPION OF GENTLEMEN

'M IN THE OFFICE OF Lord Waheed, one of the U.K.'s most successful media entrepreneurs (*The Word*, *The Big Breakfast*, and *Survivor* all made it onto screen thanks to him), the first openly gay member of Britain's House of Lords, and, of greatest significance, one of the country's biggest champions of gay rights.

His is no ordinary office. It is gloriously sybaritic. We're sitting in armchairs so plump and soft, they warrant stroking, fresh herbal tea is being served from a table upon which Lord Alli's sneaker-clad feet rest, and the walls are covered entirely with oil paintings, which, on closer inspection, are exclusively of regal-looking young men from a wing-collared past.

I tell Lord Alli that I assume the oil paintings are of some distant ancestors.

"No, nothing like that. It was my fiftieth birthday recently, and I told all my friends and family I wanted pictures of handsome eighteenth-century men. Some people like looking at flowers. I like looking at men. So I thought I'd cover my walls with pictures of them." I shouldn't be surprised by the candor of his answer. As Lord Alli made clear when he spoke during the debate in the House of Lords on

reducing the age of consent for gay sex, *"I have never been confused by my sexuality. I have only ever been confused by people's reactions to it."*

It's hard to exaggerate how much has changed in the world of gay rights since Tony Blair appointed Lord Alli to the House of Lords as its youngest member ever. From the outset, Lord Alli committed to doing everything he could to improve rights for gay people. It started with equality in the age of consent for gay sex, and then each year a new initiative: to repeal Section 28 (which banned literature about homosexuality from schools), to get same-sex parents adoption rights, legislation to prevent discrimination against homosexuals in goods and services, civil unions, gay marriage, and the right to marry in religious buildings.

When one looks at his business achievements and then these political achievements, it's a stunningly successful scorecard. And all this from a working-class kid born to two immigrant parents, who had to leave state school at sixteen to get a job in order to help keep his family fed after his dad walked out on his mom. The definitive self-made man.

So how did he do it?

> *"Well, it starts with the usual stuff that you hear: work hard, be lucky. No one is successful without those two things. But the most important thing of all is maintenance of aim. If I could pass on one thing, it is that. My business success came from maintenance of aim. I said to myself, no matter what else, I will make the best programs I can.*

My political life: maintenance of aim again—get equality for gay rights, no matter what else was going on in my life. And that's what it's about: fight the distractions, keep coming back to your thing, the thing that's most important to you."

We both reflected on that for a moment. And then he went further.

"You know, when I was younger, being gay was still treated as something to be ashamed of. It meant you had to conduct relationships in secret. It made it more difficult to have sex. I wanted equality so no one had to be ashamed. I wanted to make it easier for people to have sex. I like sex. I think people should be able to have as much sex as they want."

Maintenance of aim, right there.

"The most important thing of all is maintenance of aim. If I could pass on one thing, it is that. My business success came from maintenance of aim. I said to myself, no matter what else, I will make the best programs I can. My political life:

maintenance of aim again—
get equality for gay rights,
no matter what else was
going on in my life. And
that's what it's about: fight
the distractions, keep
coming back to your thing,
the thing that's most
important to you."

—*Lord Waheed Alli*

OLIVIA COLMAN CLEANS UP

OLIVIA COLMAN, DESCRIBED BY MERYL Streep as "divinely gifted" and one of the most loved and in-demand actresses of her generation, is telling me about her big break. I just assume she's referring to landing her first part, but it turns out she's explaining how she got her first cleaning job, the work she relied on while trying to make it in acting. *"When I was younger, me and my mum were staying at a guesthouse in Cambridge. We were regulars because it was near the hospital where my dad was. One day the owner came over and said she wanted to go away for the weekend and that I seemed dependable and looked like I needed some money, so she was going to leave me in charge to clean the rooms and run the place. And I did, and it was lovely."*

It's certainly not the path-to-stardom story I was expecting, but Olivia seems as proud of her cleaning reviews as the ones she gets for her acting. *"I was a very good cleaner; people said so. I really enjoyed the job. And I was very honest. If anyone had a secret camera, they'd know I never looked in drawers."*

This modesty and self-deprecation is typical of Olivia. When we chat, she jokingly asks me to write that she's thinner and taller in real life, which of course she is, and she has a weapons-grade loveliness about her. In person you get hit first by her disarmingly sweet, warm smile, which is at odds with the naughty words that sometimes come out of her lips, but is entirely congruent with the personality beneath. She even has a daily ritual for bringing that loveliness to life: *"I have a little rule which I've had for about twenty years now. When I leave my front door in the morning, I'm not allowed back in till I've done something nice for someone. It makes you feel nice and helps you remember you're lucky."*

Maybe those random acts of kindness are payback for something her schoolteacher did for her. Olivia had never thought of acting, but her English teacher persuaded her to audition for the school play when she was sixteen. Suffice it to say, she loved it. *"That first experience of people clapping and laughing—fucking brilliant. It was like a first try of drugs or something, it was my heroin. And I thought, if only I could earn my keep doing this, it would be amazing."*

Back then, she just assumed it was impossible. *"My mum was a nurse, my dad a surveyor; I just assumed it was a silly dream and wouldn't happen, but the older I got, the more terrible I realized I was at everything else, and that sort of helped. It meant I couldn't resort to something else."* Olivia lists the other jobs she tried to do. *"I was an awful teacher—there's a generation of children that had a lucky escape. Then I learned to type, but was a terrible secretary. Thank God for the cleaning—otherwise I would have starved."*

Unlike with the cleaning, she says there was no big break in acting. *"It's been more of a slow sizzle, really."* The first five years were tough, constantly auditioning, not getting parts. But, she says, *"It's a good thing I spent years not working, I appreciate it so much more. I hear some stories about actors behaving badly on set, and they don't realize how fucking lucky they are. I want to work with them just so I can have a word."* I have no doubt she would.

These days there's a bit less cleaning going on. She's so much in demand, directors even change parts so Olivia can play them. In the recent TV production of John le Carré's *The Night Manager,* Olivia's spy character was originally a man, but the production had the part rewritten as female. And then Olivia happily found out before the audition that she was going to have a third baby, so they rewrote the character again to match Olivia at the time of filming: six months pregnant.

I say it's a sign of how much she was wanted that they changed the spy character to a woman. As usual, she bats the praise away and says it is more a reflection of society moving on, and it was no longer acceptable to have all-male casts. What about them rewriting the part again to accommodate her unborn baby? *"Well, spies get pregnant too."*

Given her constant refusal to take credit, and her twin hall-marks of being totally grounded and lovely, her advice comes as no real surprise.

> **"If you're ever lucky enough to be successful in what you choose to do, don't ever believe your own hype, and remember it could all stop tomorrow. Do whatever you do to the best of your ability. Take the job seriously, but not yourself. And most of all, be nice to work with."**

And if you need some help with the housework, you know who to call.

"Spies get

pregnant too."

—*Olivia Colman*

THE ENDURING JAMES RHODES

T**HE FIRST TIME I HEARD** the concert pianist James Rhodes play, I didn't know who he was. The occasion wasn't even a musical event—it was more a theatrical evening celebrating the book *Letters of Note*. But onstage was a grand piano, and as the house lights went down, a skinny, scruffy man in black jeans and beaten sneakers shuffled, eyes down, over to the piano and crumpled himself over the keys under a tangle of bed-head hair. Blimey, I remember thinking to myself, he doesn't look like much of a concert pianist. I suspect most of the audience was thinking the same. But a few seconds after he started playing, we were all thinking something different, and a few mesmerizing seconds after that, we weren't thinking anything at all.

Many people say that music has changed their life, but in James's case, it literally saved his. When he was in his twenties and in a psychiatric hospital, he was found hanging by his neck from the noose he'd fashioned out of a TV cable in an enterprising and determined effort to kill himself. At his very lowest ebb following this failed suicide, a thoughtful friend smuggled into his room an iPod loaded with the *Goldberg Variations* inside a bottle of shampoo. Listening to that music gave James a respite from the demons and reminded him there may be some things worth staying alive for after all.

The reason James tied himself to that cable was ultimately due to the brutal rape he'd suffered by his gym teacher every week from the ages of five to ten, an ordeal so repeated and extreme it left him with spinal and intestinal issues, as well as deeper, more insidious mental traumas. He is therefore a man to be congratulated not just for his musical mastery (called a "genuinely poetic gift" by the *Independent* newspaper), but also for the more profound achievement of enduring those internal onslaughts to stay alive.

The other thing to say about James is he is also very funny. When we hook up at Starbucks for the first time, I proclaim it's good to meet him in person after all our texts and emails. He responds in a hushed voice, *"Fucking hell, mate, keep your voice down, people will think we're on a Tinder date."* And he gives great conversation—although, with his language, you wouldn't want your mother listening.

I tell him he completely transformed the whole room the time I heard him play, but he is having none of it: he had left feeling angry with his performance. He says the perfectionist in him always does. *"I can think I fucked it because on one note out of ten thousand I put four grams too much pressure on the key and it should have been a tiny micro-decibel quieter, but wasn't."* Such are the obsessiveness and high standards he applies in pursuit of the impossible: the perfect performance. But he's not complaining. *"Music is the one enhancer in life that doesn't have shitty side effects and doesn't cost a fortune, and I have the opportunity to surround myself in it every day. It's almost too good to be true. But it is true, so I know how lucky I am."*

His approach to classical music is deeply respectful to the composers while being refreshingly anarchic toward the industry. As likely to be playing the main stage at summer festivals as the Royal Albert Hall, he interjects performances with personal anecdotes about the composers and releases albums with bad-boy titles like *Bullets and Lullabies* and *Razor Blades Little Pills and Big Pianos*. He is an insurgent on a mission to get Bach and Beethoven to the masses.

James originally discovered the piano as a place of refuge during the early years of his secret childhood torture, but after opting for university instead of music college, he gave up the piano at eighteen and didn't touch it for ten years. Tellingly, that decade without playing was when his *"twitching, itching head gremlins"* did the most damage, culminating in the suicide attempt. But that iPod moment in treatment restored his resolve to at least get into the music industry. He set himself the goal of becoming an agent for classical pianists and contacted a well-respected agent to ask for a job. At the interview, the agent got him to play the piano. The agent listened for fifteen minutes and said he would not support James being an agent; he had to become a performer instead. And the rest of the story is coming to a cinema near you soon (his autobiography, *Instrumental*, is being turned into a movie).

I congratulate him on his success and also for the discipline he manages in his life as a concert pianist, getting up each morning to practice all day, every day. The ferocity of his response surprises me.

"That's not discipline; I love to practice. Discipline is showing up to work on time, doing the commute, paying your mortgage, getting your kids dressed, feeding them, and packing them off to school. That's discipline. That's endurance. And it's the most underrated, invisible, heroic fucking thing, just to fucking get through a day without reward or applause when all you want to do is fucking punch yourself in the face and throw yourself off a building."

Essentially, he is a man living his dream while still having to endure the nightmare. *"Look, I know how good my life looks. I'm privileged to do what I do. But I still want to die more often than I want to live, and I know I am only some meds and a couple of weeks from being back in that psychiatric ward."*

Given that he knows about living with demons better than most, I ask his advice for anyone currently in the depths of a trauma themselves.

"Well, you can say all the normal things, like talk to people, look after yourself, ask for help. But none of that makes any difference. It makes no difference at all. I guess my advice is, and it's not really advice; it's more a wish: I wish that you're lucky enough to survive when you don't want to, because things can get better. Just survive. Just survive any way you can."★

★ If you're suffering, please consider contacting the National Alliance for Mental Illness, the largest mental health organization in the United States. They will provide support and generally fight in your corner. Visit their website for more information: www.nami.org.

"Just survive.
Just survive any way
you can."

—*James Rhodes*

DAVID EAGLEMAN'S
VAST IGNORANCE

'M SITTING IN A HIP and healthy restaurant in Palo Alto, California, eating tacos and roasted Brussels sprouts with David Eagleman of Stanford University, the world's highest-profile neuroscientist, author of eight books, founder of four tech start-ups, and Silicon Valley's go-to guy for all matters to do with the brain. Or at least I thought I was, until he tells me that everything I am currently experiencing is a simulation, and there is in fact no way of knowing if it is even real. *"It looks to you like I'm sitting over here on this chair, but it is all taking place inside the darkness of your skull, which is also totally silent,"* he says in between bites of a well-laden taco. *"Your brain is just responding to the electromagnetic signals it is receiving and creating colors and shapes and putting me over here, whereas I'm actually taking place inside your head."*

He pauses, lets out a slow breath, and sums up with, *"It's so weird."*

I'm glad he added that. For one of the world's leading neuroscientists to tell you that life as we experience it is just one big simulation is a disconcerting thing to hear over a plate of tacos, compounded by the fact that, according to his theory, the tacos might not even exist. Although—it has to be said—as imaginary snacks go, they taste pretty good.

The discomfort I feel from being introduced to the truth that everything is not how it appears makes me instinctively push back, and I question is he really claiming that he doesn't exist. *"It's less that, although of course it is a real possibility that I don't, but what we can say for sure is that at the very least reality looks very different to what we think it looks like."*

So what does reality look like is my obvious next question. *"Because of the structure of our eyes, we only perceive a very thin range of all the electromagnetic radiation that is out there; as an obvious example our eyes can't see infrared light, but it still exists. The same with sound and touch, so we are only seeing and experiencing a tiny bit of reality, we're not seeing most of what is going on."*

Fortunately, this is not something we should feel bad about. In fact, according to David it is the way our brains are built, and has served us well. *"We have evolved to mainly just see what is useful. We're terrible at perceiving things at the levels of galaxies or at molecular level with atoms, our brains just aren't built for those. They're built for finding mates and food and seeing rivers and apples, the stuff that historically has helped keep us alive."*

These days, most of us are hoping for a little more from our brains, and I'm keen to get tips on what we can all do to improve our own gray matter. I ask him what he does to keep his brain working at its remarkable level.

"The secret is to keep the brain electrically active, and that comes from maintaining a level of curiosity. To get a big thrill out of

learning new things. And the good news there is there is no end to that. What we know is so shockingly little and the rest is all unchartered waters. We're standing on the edge of a pier, and it is so much fun trying to put on the next slat."

One place where David has been adding slats to the pier is within the new discipline of neurolaw where neuroscience meets the criminal justice system. David's writing and research is full of compelling examples of where a medical issue in someone's brain has caused an otherwise entirely law-abiding citizen to act criminally, the most extreme being when a previously normal forty-year-old man exhibited sudden and uncontrolled pedophilia. Under MRA scans, doctors found the presence of an egg-sized brain tumor; and the urges instantly disappeared when it was removed. The medical conclusion was the tumor had interfered with the brain's orbitofrontal cortex, which helps to regulate social behavior, and in this case led to sexual deviancy and pedophilia.

David's work in this area therefore raises questions about what we are personally responsible for, and when, if ever, we should be punished. *"In that case, the tumor was something that could be measured, and the man didn't choose to have it, so the view was it wasn't that man's fault. But most things going on in the brain we can't yet measure, many of which could be causing people to do 'bad' things, but the justice system essentially says, 'we can't see a massive tumor so we are going to punish you and make you pay for this.'"*

It is an example that illustrates a wider point related to how we think about ourselves and others and the choices we make. *"We are making decisions using a brain we didn't choose, and therefore we should have a certain humility around what we take credit and blame for. We think we are in control of ourselves most of the time, but we are mainly the product of our genes and our experiences and the effect of those experiences on our genes, and none of those are things we control."*

His position is not one of "no one should be accountable for their actions or take credit for their achievements." Rather, it is one of "let's not be too quick to judge the bad choices of others or feel too smug about our good ones." To a material extent, we are all hostage to our own unique, and mainly misunderstood, brain chemistry.

David is the first to point out that despite all the "pier building" in the world of neuroscience, we are still scratching at the surface of our understanding. Even the tools of his trade that are used to gather some semblance of what is happening inside a human being's head are extremely basic, describing an EEG machine, a staple of neurological study, as *"like looking out the window of the spaceship and trying to work out how America is doing."*

The fact that so little is clearly understood about the workings of the human brain despite its fundamental importance is one of the motivations David has for continuing to build his pier out into the unchartered waters of neuroscience. *"Take consciousness; people can bullshit all they want about it and where it comes from, but we just don't know. I'm not saying it will always be that way, hopefully we will be able to figure it out at some point, but at this point we just don't know and that's what makes our existence so weird, but for me, exciting."*

His advice captures both the sense of how far we have yet to go to unravel all the internal mysteries of what it is to be human, as well as the approach needed to help us do that:

> *"Stay keenly aware of the vastness of our ignorance. There is so much we don't know, so really put the effort into scraping at the edges of our knowledge. And remember: the most interesting, rewarding, and fascinating thing is to be wrong, to discover, 'oh, I thought I was right, but now I am seeing something that I hadn't seen before.' So be prepared to listen to that voice inside that says 'I really know very little about what's happening here.' That humility will help you learn."*

Direct from the brain of the smartest man I've ever met.

"Stay keenly aware of the vastness of our ignorance. There is so much we don't know, so really put the effort into scraping at the edges of our knowledge. And remember: the most interesting, rewarding, and fascinating thing is to be wrong."

—*David Eagleman*

ALAIN DE BOTTON, GHOST HUNTER

AS I HEAD THROUGH THE baggage area of Heathrow Airport my thoughts turn, as they always do at this point in a journey, to Alain de Botton, the writer and philosopher of everyday life. In his book *A Week at the Airport* (the title is literal; he penned the book over seven days of living, sleeping, and writing in Heathrow's Terminal 5), he describes the irrational optimism and subsequent sadness we all experience when we pass through the doors into the arrivals area and secretly scan the faces and signs of the people waiting, hoping there might be someone there for us, even though we know no one is coming. Until reading that, I thought it was just me.

It's one of a thousand examples of what the man does best: sifting through and observing, grain by grain, the fragile sand castle of the human psyche, and reassuring us that the tumble of thoughts and emotions we each experience on a typical day is normal and doesn't make us crazy. Or, at least, no more so than the next person.

His home, where we meet, is a physical manifestation of his work. It's located on a quiet street between an old church and a painter's studio, a place of philosophical respite between the worlds of art and religion, two of the many subjects on which he writes. And the quiet garden room we sit in is primed for therapeutic enquiry: two comfy chairs face one another inviting conversation, a box of tissues, and day-bed are on hand in case matters become too troubling, and a wall of books lends a reassuringly informed air to the proceedings.

Alain de Botton's output is prolific: thirteen books covering art, sex, work, relationships, travel, religion, and the other big topics life is made of. On top of that he has presented countless documentaries and set up a learning center called the School of Life, which runs courses on coping with the various dilemmas that come with being human. Alain de Botton is, without a doubt, a philosopher on a mission: *"My goal is a more emotionally literate, happier society, but one that doesn't in any way overlook the fact that life is tragic in structure."*

One of his main beliefs is that most people assume the big problems in society are political and economic, and we downplaythe significance of emotions because they are *"seen as somehow not quite serious, they're something you do at the weekend, but the more serious-sounding things like economics and politics are really, for the most part, about human emotions and human emotional functioning."*

Furthermore, it is often our emotional selves that *"cause the problems of addiction, relationship breakdown, anxiety, anger, frustration, all the other day-to-day miseries that hold people back."* And given the scale of the problems, it struck him as strange that there wasn't a single academic discipline that prepares you *"for what it means to be an emotional creature that's, a lot of the time, slightly out of control."* Hence his life's work of finding ways for us to guide and console ourselves.

So was this always his calling? Did he set out from an early age to help navigate the human condition?

"Look, I'm a timid, obedient soul by nature. I wanted to have a normal job. I was a swot, I liked obeying orders, I liked to fit in. But I knew it was all fake, I knew it was all rubbish. I was just doing it to please my very demanding family and to be a good chap, but as I grew older, the idea of a normal job, of being a management accountant or whatever, increasingly made me feel dead inside. But it left me with a crisis as I left university, thinking, so what now?"

His view is that society places a lot of pressure on people to know what they want to do and that pressure can be disabling. While some lucky people do know from an early age what they want to do, and others are happy just to do a job if it pays the bills, there is a large, third category of people who feel, *"I know there's something I want to do, but I don't know what it is yet. And the world can be quite impatient with those people. Unless you can say to the world 'I want to do a specific thing,' we're steamrollered."*

So Alain de Botton's advice on how to lead a more nourishing life speaks directly to those people in that third category: *"Find the thing that drives you. It's not easy. Most of us are not obvious to ourselves. But we occasionally pick up indistinct signals, some kind of vague longing, from something that feels like a ghost-self, deep within us, something that refuses to die but is not quite alive either. That ghost is our true self, trying to come out. Listen out for it. We have to turn our ghost-self into a real person. We need to bring the ghost to life."*

I ask for tips for those people trying to track down their ghost. Surprisingly, envy, pessimism, and death are all to be enlisted to help with the ghost hunt.

"Analyze what you are envious of. It is very unlikely we actually envy a whole person; if you break it down you'll find you actually just envy specific attributes of them, say their approach to graphic design or their ability to make cakes, and you can build up, from an analysis of your envy, a model of your ideal self."

You'll also need to experiment and try new things, so a background pessimism helps take the pressure off. *"'It's all going to go wrong' is a useful starting point, allowing us to make peace with failure. I've calmed myself down in risky ventures many times with a sense of 'Oh fuck it, it may all blow up, but that's OK.'"*

Finally, you can use death to help, albeit indirectly. *"One doesn't want to frighten people but, obviously, life is extremely short and reminding ourselves of that should invigorate us and shake us from a kind of lethargy when we are searching."*

And if after all that you still don't know what to do, then don't worry. Alain says it could be that the angst-ridden, existential philosophers of the mid-twentieth century were right all along. They believed we're all shooting in the dark when it comes to making the big decisions about what to do with our lives and we shouldn't expect to know, or even enjoy finding out. Ultimately they just accepted the wisdom of Solon instead, who decreed: Let no man be called happy before his death.

Cheery lot, these philosophers.

"We have to turn our ghost-self into a real person. We need to bring the ghost to life."

—*Alain de Botton*

RUBY WAX'S FUNNY MIND

"*I* COULDN'T STOP. *I WAS EVEN doing gags during my Caesarean.*" Ruby Wax, actress, writer, and comedian, is recounting the unhealthy pressure she used to feel to be funny. She's not complaining, just explaining one of the downsides of being a professional comedian: the expectation that you'll always clown around and be amusing.

What compounded the pressure to be funny was Ruby's history of heavy bouts of depression, a reality she felt she had to deny, given her day job. This hiding of her illness even reached its logical extreme—she once discharged herself from a mental treatment center where she was a patient to go interview someone for a TV show, then returned to the hospital that evening. *"When I got back the inmates looked at me and said, 'Are you crazy?' Which was high praise coming from them."*

She is still a very funny lady, but she has a second, more serious focus these days: campaigning for greater mental health and destigmatizing the issue. It's an area she knows a lot about, not just from her own experiences but also because in a bid to understand the illness that would periodically floor her she did a Masters in mindfulness-based cognitive behavioral therapy at Oxford University and made it her mission to unpick what was going on when depression strikes.

An American now resident in the United Kingdom, Ruby didn't intend for this new path to make her a poster child for mental health, but she became one, quite literally. A Comic Relief–funded initiative to promote awareness of mental illness placed posters all over the London Underground which featured Ruby saying she'd experienced depression. She was originally shocked by the attention: *"I thought it looked like a showbiz poster, but I decided to piggyback on it by writing a show on mental illness and pretending that I did the whole thing on purpose."* She performed the show for the first time in The Priory treatment clinic, where she had previously recovered from a breakdown, and because it was so well received she toured other mental health institutes throughout the country. Books and more shows followed, each with a purpose of providing respite, insight, and counsel for people with the anxieties and issues of the modern-day mind.

After twenty-five years of making people laugh on television, she says these days she would rather be in the smoking room of mental institutes talking to the patients she now refers to as *"my people."* And while it would be difficult to think of anyone who has done more to get mental health issues out into the open, she's not done yet. Her latest initiative is to roll out Frazzled Cafés, walk-in meetings held at Marks & Spencer stores across the country where people who are on *"the cusp of burning out, who are feeling isolated"* can meet up, support each other, and share stories.

It all fits with Ruby's gloriously open-minded, open-hearted approach to mental illness: get it out in the open, get it talked about. Stop suffering it in silence and feeling like you have to hide it. She knows there are no easy solutions, and while she advocates daily exercises of mindfulness (*"you have to practice, you don't get a six-pack just by thinking about one"*) she's also pragmatic about taking meds if they work for you: *"If you were a diabetic, you would take the insulin."*

She does still get hit with depression sometimes, the difference being it now lasts weeks rather than months, and she is better at noticing it and dealing with it. In terms of the advice she gives, it neither downplays nor overstates the significance of how you respond to mental illness.

> **"Don't get depressed about the depression. Depression can bring with it a sense of shame, that we beat ourselves up for having it, that we're ashamed to have this vulnerability. But you have to forgive yourself and allow yourself to feel it. It's normal and it's natural and a basic human foible that affects one in four of us. Take strength and solidarity from those numbers."**

IN THE DARK
WITH SHEP GORDON

W E'RE ON A CRUISE SHIP out of Miami. It's midnight. There are more than 3,000 entrepreneurs on board. It's billed as a seminar at sea; in reality, it's a party weekend thinly disguised as a conference. But most of us, for once, are forgoing the bars and clubs and restaurants. Instead, we're packed into the main auditorium, listening reverently to one man in shorts, sandals, and a Bermuda shirt talk onstage. That man is Shep Gordon.

There are only two types of people in the world: those who love Shep Gordon and those who don't know who he is. For those in the second camp, the best place to start is *Supermensch: The Legend of Shep Gordon*, the documentary made by his friend Mike Myers. It covers the life and times of one of the most loved men and managers in Hollywood, who started his career masterminding the infamous reputation of Alice Cooper in the 1970s, and who now acts as close advisor to the Dalai Lama, via pretty much everyone else of note.

The documentary is a master class in hedonism, friendship, drug consumption, management, and spirituality. It seems no one has led a faster life, a fuller life, a life more dedicated to making other people happy. It's like watching a video made for a loved one's milestone birthday, in which every Hollywood star you can think of is expressing their love and telling naughty stories.

I caught Shep after his speech, which had been peppered with anecdote after anecdote of eyebrow-raising excess, profound Buddhist insights, and brilliant juicy gossip. And through it all, he came across as a man who is at peace with himself. Who is happy. Who is doing what he wants to do. He says as much when passing on his advice.

"My advice is follow your bliss."

I ask him to expand.

"If you want to have a good life, you have to find out, and then only do, what makes you happy."

And if you don't know what that is?

"Then my advice is this: go into a room, a dark room, by yourself, for at least thirty minutes every day. And sit there in the dark and think. And keep doing that, keep going into that room every day, until you have worked out what it is that makes you happy."

I asked him, other than sitting in dark rooms, what is *his* bliss.

"My bliss is making other people happy. I've been trying to do that all my life."

An answer that chimed with everything we had seen and heard. As did his final comment.

"And now I am going to make myself happy by going back to my cabin, sitting on my balcony, and rolling myself a nice big spliff."
Shep Gordon: supermensch.

"Follow your bliss....
If you want to have
a good life, you have
to find out, and then
only do, what makes
you happy."

—*Shep Gordon*

ABSOLUTELY LUMLEY

'M AT AN AWARDS DO and the god of seating plans has smiled benevolently upon me. I'm seated next to Joanna Lumley, one of the UK's most loved actresses, and also one of the country's most prolific and effective activists. To talk to, she is as one would expect: warm, inclusive, crush-inducing. But with these soft-edged charms come inspiring, hard-edged principles: a sense of civic duty, of justice, of doing the right thing. She is a heady combination of warm heart and iron will. Which explains that while her TV and film work would be a career to be proud of in itself, it is her commitments and contributions off-screen that are the most remarkable.

Take the plan for a Garden Bridge across the Thames River in London, a concept as beautiful as it is original. A vision known and loved throughout most of London. Just like Joanna Lumley. But what is less known is that it was entirely her idea, a concept she dreamt up and then agitated to set the wheels in motion. And woe be tide those that currently stand in her way of making it happen.

Or look at the issue of Nepalese Gurkha veterans (who served in the British armed forces before 1997), who have historically been denied the right to settle in the United Kingdom after fighting for the country—a morally bankrupt decision and one that needed reversing. It was an unfashionable and unfabulous fight, but one that Joanna Lumley took on unreservedly, using her charm, celebrity, conviction, and sheer dogged resilience until the victory was achieved and those rights installed.

In short, she is no ordinary woman.

And when I give a short speech later at the awards do and say I've been sitting next to Joanna Lumley, the audience erupts in applause: everyone in the room loves her.

There was therefore a synchronicity to the advice she gave me.

> *"The secret, darling, is to love everyone you meet. From the moment you meet them. Give everyone the benefit of the doubt. Start from a position that they are lovely and that you will love them. Most people will respond to that and be lovely and love you back and it becomes a self-fulfilling prophecy, and you can then achieve the most wonderful things."*

Then she leaned forward and whispered in my ear.

> *"But get rid of any of the bastards that let you down."*

As I said: warm heart, iron will.

"The secret, darling, is to love everyone you meet. From the moment you meet them. Give everyone the benefit of the doubt."

—*Joanna Lumley*

JAMES CORDEN,
MAN OF THE WORLD

LSTREE FILM STUDIOS IN NORTH London arguably
lacks some of the glamour and pizzazz of its Hollywood
equivalents, but on the plus side, it does have a local
Nando's. It's also where the eleventh series of *A League of Their Own* is being recorded, hosted by the U.K.'s hottest acting/presenting/writing/carpooling export, James Corden.

I'm shown into his dressing room in the afternoon, before that evening's show. The TV is on. James is sitting on a sofa watching his mate Andy Murray's Wimbledon semifinal, and he invites me to come join him. We both become transfixed by the game, sitting side by side, with our feet up on the coffee table, passing the occasional comment on the match. Then, after a little while, some Nando's arrives, and I find myself having a TV dinner with the biggest guy on it right now.

It has to be said: James Corden makes a great TV-dinner companion. He has that indefinable quality where you relax as soon as you meet him. His talent for singing, acting, writing, presenting, and even dancing would be intimidating in someone else, but his "good guy" vibes are even stronger. You instinctively feel he is in your corner. Or, in this case, corner sofa.

That easygoing, humble charm is part of the reason the biggest names in entertainment all want to appear on his internet-breaking U.S. TV show. Adele rode with him in Carpool Karaoke, Justin Bieber dressed in James's clothes and copresented the program, and Tom Hanks reenacted nine of his most famous movie scenes with James for the launch episode. Celebrities don't even do it to plug their latest whatevers—they just want to do the show.

No one appreciates America's triple A-list making him feel so welcome more than James. *"I don't quite know what I've done to deserve such brilliant memories. Just last week I was driving around the White House with Michelle Obama and I thought to myself, 'I don't think this would have happened if I'd stayed in High Wycombe.'"*

A big factor in the A-list's involvement is that the guests feel safe. They know with James they're not going to end up looking stupid, unless they want to. *"There's a degree of trust that comes from the fact that I am not interested in making anyone do anything but shine. And we always start from what is going to bring the most joy."*

Joy creation is an apt description for what James does for a living. And for us, the viewer, that joy comes partly from seeing that James himself is loving every second of it. *"I learned that from my time on Broadway in* The History Boys. *People always said they loved that we looked like we were having a blast, so I thought to myself, if that's what people like, then why don't I aim to actually have a good time rather than just act like I am."*

In fact, enjoying the experience comes relatively easily. *"I just don't remember a time when I didn't want to perform, or, let's be honest, show off in some capacity."* But the quality of the output requires a serious work ethic. James loves partnering up with the greats because it helps him raise his own game. He recounts how Tom Hanks flew in a day early to rehearse with James over and over again for the launch show. *"I just couldn't stop going, 'Thank you so much for doing this,' and he said, 'James, this is show business. And show business is about working really hard, because the harder you work, the quicker you can forget about it.' And I thought, 'Oh my God. You're so right.' The things you work hard on and do well, they never play on your mind; it's the ones where you didn't quite give it your all that plague you after."* It's a principle that holds true in life generally.

Gavin and Stacey is one of the things James has never had to give another thought to. Every line he and his cowriter Ruth Jones wrote, and the delivery of each one of them, stands the test of time, as evidenced by the *Friends*-esque continual repeats on British satellite TV. I tell him that, to me, the series quietly and brilliantly captures all the beautiful idiosyncrasies and nonsense of being British, and that if an alien species wanted to understand our country, you could tell them to just have a cup of tea and watch all twenty episodes.

James pushes back a little on this and says he hopes the program is more universal than British; he would *"prefer it if someone said this is a story about people who fell in love, and because of that, their families changed and then their family's family changed, and that happens all over the world."* That highlights another reason for his success: the content James creates has universal appeal—Carpool Karaoke is as joyful to people in Iran as it is to people in Iceland or Italy.

This truth that James's success illustrates—that no matter where people are, they find the same jokes funny, the same stories interesting, and want to see the same people in front of the camera—informs in him a bigger worldview. *"We're all so much more alike than different. And if you don't necessarily think of yourself as being particular to one country but as a citizen of the world, then so many issues are reduced. For example, you don't think firstly how can we reduce immigration into our country—you instead think how can we make all of our countries better."*

He tells a sweet story of passing this one-world ethos on to his five-year-old son, who'd asked him recently why it was important to recycle.

"I said, 'Imagine if you found a floating ball that's twenty-five foot by twenty-five foot, and not only is it floating but it rotates slightly, and if you get closer to it, you can see loads of tiny creatures on it walking around. And if you look even more closely, not one of them is the same, they are all completely unique, and they hug each other and love each other and build amazing things. And if then someone came along and went, "Let's just pour some acid on this bit of the ball here, and cover this bit with loads of rubbish," people would be up in arms and say we have to protect this forever, wouldn't they? Well, our Earth is that ball.' And he was just like, 'Yeah, OK, Dad. Can we go outside and play now?'"

Given that he is passing on wisdom, I ask him for his best piece of advice. In response, he advocates the importance of finding one's "thing."

> **"There is an inner steel that comes from knowing you're good at something. It might be plumbing or building tables or driving a cab or whatever, but being able to say 'When it comes to this, I know what I'm doing' is good for one's**

confidence. So my advice to someone younger is search for the thing you're good at and don't stop."

After passing on this advice, he then candidly recounts how finding his thing helped him find his inner steel and deal with times he had getting picked on as a kid.

"I remember being at school, thinking, yes, you can run faster than me and you're stronger than me and you're better at maths than me and you're better at playing the piano, but when the school play comes around, you're nowhere. And it stopped me from feeling too bullied and outcast."

That sense of self, of having something he was good at, emboldened him. And he finishes by telling me of the time he went to the career advisor, and they asked what he was going to do when he was older. *"I said, 'I'm going to be an actor,' and they said, 'No, you might want to be an actor, but you will need something else.' And I just said, 'No, I am going to be an actor,' and committed myself fully to that. After all, if you don't give up, you'll never fail."*

It's a commitment that clearly paid off, and we viewers get to enjoy his success just as much as he does.

AT ONE WITH THE DALAI LAMA

'M BACKSTAGE WAITING TO MEET with His Holiness, the
14th Dalai Lama. The hallway is packed on either side with
bodyguards in black suits, producers with clipboards, and
charity folk waiting their turn to meet with the spiritual leader
of Tibet. While the place is busy, the atmosphere is noticeably
relaxed and convivial. Even the bouncers radiate a peaceful vibe,
despite their "but don't even think about it" faces.

The fact that the Dalai Lama's entourage is so calm should
come as no surprise. His Holiness is, quite literally, the human
manifestation of peace and compassion, and according to
Buddhist teachings a fully realized being reborn into the world
to help all living things. To be this close to his presence brings
out the best in everyone.

Earlier in the day I listened to him speak onstage. He sits
on a grandfatherly armchair, with his simple maroon robes
hugged around him. The room fully silent, we communally
absorb his profound and essential message: Simply put, the
twentieth century was a period marked by unimaginable wars,
violence, genocides, inequality, and climate change. And
anyone who has lived through these times has a duty of care
to help the generations born in the twenty-first century avoid

the same mistakes. After all, these were all problems caused by man, so we have the power to stop them happening again.

According to the Dalai Lama, the key to preventing such destructive tendencies is for us all to develop a sense of inner peace. That's because the negative actions of war and violence, and the harmful emotions of fear and greed, never come from someone with a calm mind, an insight that the Dalai Lama points out is verified by all relevant sources, be they the science of neurology (one of the Dalai Lama's key interests), our own common sense, or the ancient teachings.

It is a narrative that is beguilingly simple, and ultimately so hard to disagree with. The way His Holiness delivers the message helps land it. While he may be talking about matters of the utmost seriousness, his style is infused with joy and warmth, interspersed with irreverence and humor, and quickly accompanied by his own infectious chuckle. It is as if he is saying, we may be talking about life and death, but we don't have to take it so seriously.

When I meet him in person later on, the same magical blend of science and spirituality, mysticism and mischief continues. He comes into the room and sits opposite me. Gaze steady, ready to listen. The calmness radiating from him more than neutralizes the nervousness radiating from me. I put forward my question about his single most important piece of advice; and then after a few seconds of thought, he answers in a single word: *"Oneness,"* he says in a definitive tone, and then sits back in his chair, silent.

I now find myself in a slight quandary. I have consulted one of the most revered spiritual leaders on Earth. He has listened to my question and given his response. It is without doubt a deeply profound answer, and that single word contains a lifetime of wisdom. But if I am being really honest, I was secretly hoping for something, well, a bit longer.

I don't know the etiquette on asking spiritual leaders to try again, so I too decide to stay quiet. And we sit opposite one another in silence, but comfortably so.

Fortunately, His Holiness decides to expand. *"If you go to the deeper level, we are all part of the same human family. We are all part of humankind. And whether we like it or not, we all have to live on the same planet. We are all interdependent. East depends on West. North depends on South. We need to place less emphasis on our secondary differences, our religions, our nation states, and more emphasis on the fact that ultimately we are the same. That is how we can live much more peacefully."*

Again, it is masterly in its simplicity. Ambitious in its scope, it is ultimately incontestable in its logic. If only, I find myself thinking.

How do we encourage such a sense and understanding of oneness, I ask keenly. *"By education,"* he says. Then something unexpected happens. The Dalai Lama leans forwards, raises his hand, and raps me really quite hard on my forehead with his knuckles, and repeats, *"By education."* And then His Holiness sits back again, chuckling; and I find myself doing the same.

For one glorious moment there we are, sitting opposite each other, giggling. And I without doubt feel an indefinable sense of oneness with him. And it has to be said, a slightly dull ache on my forehead.

"Oneness."

—*Dalai Lama*

MUCHAS GRACIAS

THE BIGGEST THANKS GO TO Head Coach Jamie Bada Byng, a man with enough energy to power all of West London and who most of the time seems to be actually doing so. He is the first and last word in passion, insight, and encouragement, a door opener without equal, and the man to call if you ever want chicken wings for breakfast.

My soothsaying agent, Tony Topping, was a consistent source of erudite advice and wise counsel. And he was plain-speaking enough to remind me of the basics of writing a book, not least that I would have to actually write it.

A big thank-you to Sophie Sutcliffe, who, while heavily preggers, worked the phone lines and the inboxes and got us some great participants. And thanks to little Poppy for allowing her mom to do so.

Francesca Zampi, my erstwhile partner in crime and fellow hustler, was super encouraging from the get-go and opened her address book to me. Likewise Kim Chappell, who was an absolute *tour de force* of contacts, good vibes, and emails, and a lovely person to drink tea with. Lucy McIntyre was a star in every sense and opened up New York, and Lizzie Ball, Nick Clegg, and

Alain de Botton were super kind and helpful in getting me in front of people as remarkable as themselves.

The teams at Canongate and Chronicle Books have been an unfailingly professional, fun, and smart group of people to work with and have made all of it a pleasure, with special thanks to Jo Dingley, Rafi Romaya, Anna Frame, Jenny Fry, Lara Gardellini, and Jenny Todd at Canongate; and Evelyn Liang, Vanessa Dina, Marie Oishi, Freesia Blizard, Meghan Legg, Maggie Edelman, Alexandra Brown, and Christine Carswell at Chronicle Books.

Sam Kerr, as you will have seen with your own eyes, is a brilliant artist whose portraits have totally been the making of the book.

Behind the scenes, there have been some people I may never meet but remain forever grateful to: the transcribers, especially our number-one, Callum Crowe, and the delightful open-all-hours Debs Warner as copyeditor in chief.

I am, of course, super grateful to each participant who lent their time, story, and, most importantly, advice to the project.

And in terms of the gushy bits, an unconditional thank-you to my mum and dad, who to this day, and despite the many remarkably wise people I have met, continue to be the source of the best advice I have ever had, and to Nadia and Bay Rose, the result of listening to that advice and the people I have been waiting my whole life to meet.

INDEX

BEHIND THE BOOK

Richard Reed, entrepreneur, philanthropist, and radio presenter, is the cofounder of Innocent Drinks, the Innocent Foundation, and JamJar Investments, as well as the founder of Art Everywhere. He lives in the United Kingdom.

www.innocentfoundation.org
www.jamjarinvestments.com
www.arteverywhere.org.uk

Samuel Kerr's work spans portraiture, print design, art direction, and brand identities for clients such as Coca-Cola, Gillette, Paul Smith, *Time* magazine, *GQ*, and *The Guardian*. He lives in the United Kingdom.

www.samuelkerr.co.uk